RAVES FOR *THE JUSTIN MICHAEL METHOD*

"Justin's approach to prospecting has not only revolutionized my personal pipeline (14 cold outbound meetings) in less than 2 weeks using the JMM (Justin Michael Method). But he has also managed to build an incredible community that I look to outside of work for life advice."

– Luke Ruffing, Account Executive, Reveal

"In one month, Justin transformed my sales skills from knowing virtually nothing to booking meetings and closing deals with top decision-makers. Working with Justin is a no-brainer."

– Tavis Lochhead, Co-Founder, Kadoa

"Justin's approach to pipeline generation is disruptive and extremely effective. No one I've met has more experience in the trenches and practical expertise in outbound than this man. Salespeople can quickly pick up and run with the methodology with minimal effort as it's been designed to be scalable and adaptable to each individual's unique style. Justin explains the why behind everything, and by helping sellers to understand and then tap into human psychology, it's no surprise that the JMM gets results."

– Kieran Krohn, Senior Sales Manager, HubSpot

"Since working with Justin, my team has made a 180% increase in closed business - 2.2MM - and 300% increase in validated pipeline. He is no doubt the best of the best (of all the rest). Great investment. As a profoundly innovative leader, Justin always focuses on what is important to the people and business goals he serves. He is meticulous and vigilant in obtaining critical insights for B2B leaders through collaborative assessment, a guided self-reflection, perspective and change support. He is an outstanding role model, a consummate teacher and business leader; one that applies common sense excellence in his standards. I admire and respect Justin for achieving at a world class level and doing so through worthy core values. I strongly recommend him to any business wanting to make critical B2B improvements in productivity and business growth."

– Mark C. Green, Chief Revenue Office, TeleVox Pharmaceutical & Payor

"Justin Michael is the Obi-Wan Kenobi of opening conversations. Justin trains you to think holistically rather than relying on tactics, stratagems, or playbooks. By drawing on fundamental insights from neuroscience, Game Theory, and negotiation, Justin contextualizes the sales process against a much more critical skillset: Understanding what it means to be, in the world of Arnold Schwarzenegger, 'useful' - a selfless professional advisor acting in the best interests of the people whose lives they touch. There is nobody better."

– Charles Needham, Business Development, Revenue Drivers

"Mindset is key. I understood to get to the next tier that my efforts and progress hinged on new tactics and strategies from someone killing it. I was hunting 'secrets from the field' ...not just more sales training. So, I teamed up with Justin, a real powerhouse, who not only is equipped with a plethora of wisdom from his new book and record of accomplishments in his business ventures, but he is an exceptional guide spotting unexplored capabilities that even I was unaware of. He illuminated my path helping me unlock sections of dormant talent that had gone unnoticed, aiding me with the ability to completely knock the door down and demolish boundaries. The impact of this partnership on my mindset, concentration, and perspectives has been profound. It has infused additional meaning and purpose in selling to executive-level decision-makers. Such an invaluable foundation is irreplaceable."

– Marc Periou, DM Executive, SAP

"My reps are seeing an immediate uplift in positive response rates, phone+call+social, after implementing the JMM framework. Justin is hyper-engaged with everyone who takes his course. His collaborative, interactive style creates the environment of him speaking WITH us, not AT us."

– Adam Tan, Sales Dev, Backblaze

"Calling Justin Michael the best sales coach in the world is a massive understatement."

– Scott Hennessy, Managing Director, The HD Agency

"Disorganized. Cold-call reluctance. Unsure of where to even start. To pure, profound confidence. A deep understanding of the polarity shift, with the ability to predict to a tee what exactly will happen next. I'm not talking- they are."

– David Catalano, Outbound Sales Development Rep, ZoomInfo

"I recommend Justin to C-Levels and companies that want more revenue fast. Justin is a genius regarding sales, sales methodologies, automation, and sales tech. He will catch you up on what's trending and, more important, working right now (not five years ago). Justin has a unique approach and sometimes mind-bending, thought-provoking ideas and methods."

– Dennis O'Hagan, CEO, The Rainmakers

"I recommend that anybody in the business development position connect, follow and contact Justin Michael ASAP. He will change your life."

– Thomas Fuller, Business Development Advisor, GSA National

"Justin Michael is a sales savant! He has pressure tested what does and doesn't work for the last 20 years. In the crowded field of Sales Mentors - Justin's analytical, neuro-science-driven approach is King - because it takes you into the mindset of the executives you are helping."

– Tom Tobin, Senior Account Executive, Kofax

"Justin Michael has helped change the game for me. He came along at a time in my life when I needed to reinvent myself and make some significant changes. Justin has helped me in this area so much, and primarily he has given me more confidence and has provided me with some great insight."

"When I reached out to Justin for personalized coaching, I was impressed by his genuine desire to help me improve. He cares deeply about his client's success on both a personal and professional level. During our time together, Justin pushed me far outside my comfort zone to build an effective daily prospecting routine. His breadth of sales knowledge is impressive, and he skillfully tailored his advice to my specific industry and role. Justin also went above and beyond as a mentor. He provided invaluable guidance on sales techniques, mindset, motivation, and addressing the inner roadblocks that hold people back. Thanks to his coaching, I now have a repeatable system for outbound that has already led to valuable new connections."

"Justin is BRILLIANT in regards to revenue operations and sales velocity. I have zero doubt, he is one of the best in the world at this time."

"If you want to take your sales career to the next level, Justin is the one to turn to. He has a proven track record in the tech industry and can guide you toward unlocking unlimited potential. Justin's coaching methods, known as the JMM Methodology, have consistently doubled and even tripled revenue for individuals and teams."

– Joshua Reed, Account Executive, Foxpass

"At the time of this writing, I've been working with Justin for just 10 days. In that time, using his method I was able to land 2 meetings with highly qualified clients despite having very limited sales experience. I feel like I've learned more about sales in 10 days with Justin than in 4 years in business school."

– Florian Decludt, Founder, Alexis Growth

"I've hired Justin to work with my BDR teams at two different companies. He is great with the reps! He doesn't just tell them what they should be doing, he actually gets involved in their daily activities, helping them with their scripts, emails, objection handling, personalization of message, etc. His method works. At both companies, we saw a definite uptick in the number of qualified outbound leads per week. I'd definitely recommend Justin to any company looking to level up their BDR game. Even if you have a BDR manager in place, Justin can complement that person with his real-world experience and daily 'strength training' of the team."

– Scott Frymire, SVP Corporate Marketing, Odessa

"Justin can naturally identify outbound weaknesses and quickly provide effective solutions that are scalable. I felt like Justin had transferred me all of his advanced outbound/sales knowledge in a way that I could easily understand so I could tailor it into my own work. He goes above and beyond with tech stacks, onboarding processes, sales, email strategies, cold calling, sequencing, customer service, and how to scale a team around outbound."

– Caleb Sinn, Founder, Social

SALES SUPERPOWERS:

A NEW OUTBOUND OPERATING SYSTEM TO DRIVE EXPLOSIVE PIPELINE GROWTH (JUSTIN MICHAEL METHOD 1.0)

JUSTIN MICHAEL

Sales Superpowers: A New Outbound Operating System To Drive Explosive Pipeline Growth (Justin Michael Method 1.0)

Author: Justin Michael

Jones Media Publishing
10645 N. Tatum Blvd. Ste. 200-166
Phoenix, AZ 85028
www.JonesMediaPublishing.com

Disclaimer:

The author strives to be as accurate and complete as possible in the creation of this book, notwithstanding the fact that the author does not warrant or represent at any time that the contents within are accurate due to the rapidly changing nature of the Internet.

While all attempts have been made to verify information provided in this publication, the Author and the Publisher assume no responsibility and are not liable for errors, omissions, or contrary interpretation of the subject matter herein. The Author and Publisher hereby disclaim any liability, loss or damage incurred as a result of the application and utilization, whether directly or indirectly, of any information, suggestion, advice, or procedure in this book. Any perceived slights of specific persons, peoples, or organizations are unintentional.

In practical advice books, like anything else in life, there are no guarantees of income made. Readers are cautioned to rely on their own judgment about their individual circumstances to act accordingly. Readers are responsible for their own actions, choices, and results. This book is not intended for use as a source of legal, business, accounting or financial advice. All readers are advised to seek the services of competent professionals in legal, business, accounting, and finance field.

Printed in the United States of America

ISBN: 978-1-948382-68-7 paperback

Thanks for reading!

Get our special reader resources and bonus training by going to:

SalesSuperpowers.com/bonus

Contents

FOREWORD BY TONY HUGHES

Let's face it – the world is going crazy. Technology is advancing faster than most people can understand, let alone master. Some worry about whether the salesbots are coming to disrupt the sales profession. Should you be concerned as a seller about AI-driven technology replacing you? Maybe; but the first thing to worry about is another tech-savvy human salesperson leaving you in their dust with a high technology quotient (TQ) outperforming you at every level.

Most sales organizations are fumbling their technology stack, most of which is under-utilized by bewildered sellers. Marketers and salespeople trying to automate outbound are accidentally "burning through their lists." They're damaging their brand and losing opportunities with poor messaging, inadequate personalization, and ineffective execution.

Buyers are being bombarded with "spam" and they are increasingly deadened to sales outreach. Their email inbox is clogged, their LinkedIn InMail is filled with clumsy noise and disingenuous attempts to connect with them. How do sellers break through the white wall of noise surrounding hard to reach buyers?

To succeed in the 'new economy' sellers must address the key elements of success. First, nail the narrative (value message), then create engagement across multiple channels of communication.

With this foundation, you're ready to level up with systems, technology and automation. Teams can become cyborg armies of effectiveness.

Justin Michael has cracked the code for bringing all of these elements together.

I've known Justin Michael for a decade and collaborated with him on two of my books, *COMBO Prospecting* and *Tech-Powered Sales*. He is the real deal in every way. Justin is a Ninja black belt in sales systems and tech-stack effectiveness, and an insanely gifted sales copywriter. Add to this his ability to blend marketing and sales for outbound that creates inbound, along with his knowledge in harnessing the power of buyer trigger events, and you have someone truly unique.

Justin has coached and mentored hundreds of people and they attest to the power of his system for driving results. This book is dripping in actionable ideas that can work for you if you adopt a growth mindset for building and scaling sales success as you step out of your comfort zone.

The Death and Rebirth of Outbound

It's 2023 and based on Bridge Group research, the "SDR" may be doomed to disappear within 5-10 years if nothing changes.

Sales Development Representatives (SDRs) are 71% less effective at connecting with decision-makers than they were 10 years ago. They're making 55% more attempts per contact (calls, emails, Linkedin touches, etc.) but they're getting 55% fewer responses: connected calls, and email replies.

There's clearly something wrong, and it's not just a sales problem - it's an issue that spreads from something deeper, our human psychology, the way we approach life, and the way we communicate.

You've probably noticed it yourself. The world has changed drastically in such a short space of time. We're living in a world that's somehow more connected, and simultaneously disconnected than ever before.

Studies tell us we spend 75% of our working hours glued to our screens, primarily the ones we keep in our pockets. Relationships, work, and information all flow through the same app-enabled devices we keep with us 24 hours a day.

Product managers and growth hackers constructed the most effective dopamine chains possible, keeping us tethered to our devices, and attention spans are waning as a result. Despite social media, we're becoming less social. In an era of endless communication methods, meaningful conversations are disappearing.

The world is more distracted and disengaged than ever, and salespeople are feeling the impact. After all, a huge part of what you do is "connect." Salespeople are masters of relationships, communication, and engagement.

But in a world where everything is fighting against you for your customer's attention, how do you break through the deafening noise?

The answer is simpler than it seems: flip the script.

It's time for a new approach to sales and communication - a new method that harnesses the building blocks of the mind, and the idiosyncrasies of the human condition. We need to go back to the basics, while simultaneously embracing the future, to thrive in a world of complex contradictions.

I've named this strategy the "Justin Michael Method," for simplicity's sake, but I encourage you to look at my name as a placeholder. Take the lessons you learn here, and use them to build your own "[Your name here] Method."

This is a guide built for you, the next generation of salesperson - the phoenix ready to rise from the ashes. So read on if you're tired of disconnection, and want a clear path to the promised land of overflowing pipeline in sales.

— In collaboration with Scott Martinis

A New Outbound Operating System

"Justin's results as a client acquisition coach are nothing short of spectacular. ROI is lightning fast."

– Zach Selch, Principal, Global Sales Mentor

I could start this guide with a million promises, waxing poetic about the life-changing advice I've given my clients over the years. But the reality is, as you'll learn through these pages, what you get from this work depends on you.

What I can tell you is everything you're dreaming of **is possible**.

Want to improve your ROI by 100,000 times? Unlock limitless leads and opportunities, or just get more joy out of your career? You can, and you will. The advice I'm giving you here stems from strategies that have already earned me, and my coaching clients millions of dollars.

But, as Morpheus said: "I can only show you the door. You're the one who has to walk through it."

The problem most of the sellers I talk to have is simple, they don't know where to start. We all want exponential growth, high revenues, great achievements. But figuring out how to turn that little acorn of potential into an oak tree can seem like trying to dissect magic.

That's particularly true when all of the guidance we currently have in the sales landscape seems designed for a different era - a world we're no longer living in.

For too long, sellers have been drowning in a cacophony of hollow advice from inexperienced, fame-seeking dark gurus in the LinkedIn feed echo chamber. The world has become obsessed with saccharine quick fixes, magic bullet courses, and gimmicks over deep business acumen.

As I promised in the prologue to this book, I'm here to introduce you to a new approach. I built this work with feedback from you, the sales community, insights from countless experts, and years of research, to be the guide I wish I had 22 years ago, when I first started, and the guide countless new salespeople need now, in the evolving era of outbound.

Together, we're not just going to go "back to the basics." We're going to rethink the entire sales methodology, from a new perspective, focused on human connection.

We're going to explore the secrets to my success, and the strategies that have helped my clients achieve their goals, and discuss why they worked, and why they'll continue to work decades from now.

The onus is on you to do the work, take the lessons you learn and activate them. But you don't have to go it alone. I hope, by the end of this journey, you'll think of me, and this work as your very own Jiminy Cricket. The angel on your shoulder constantly pushing you to rethink, reconsider, and revive your sales strategy.

If you're ready to dive in, feel free to skip forward a couple of pages - I won't hold it against you. But if you want a quick peek behind the curtain, here's everything you need to know about where this book actually came from.

BEHIND THE "JUSTIN MICHAEL METHOD"

Let's face it. Sales has always been challenging.

You know it. I know it. Even your prospects know it.

But things have been getting tougher lately. Economic downturns, macro shifts, evolutions in AI - heck, even the pandemic - they've all made life harder for us as salespeople.

But what if, in the face of all these unpredictable events, you could still reach your goals? What if the path to success doesn't lie in constantly "reacting" to challenges as they emerge with the latest trends suggested by "gurus" on LinkedIn, but in a proactive approach that leverages something infinite and consistent - the human psyche?

The ideas and concepts that are shared in this book are synthesized out of 100s of ideas crowd tested after I made them open source. They stem in part from the *Codices*, as we call them at HYPCCCYCL (hypcccycl.com/codexes) - the methodologies that caused a tidal wave on Reddit. But, they also come from something simpler - the universal truths I've discovered through my life as a coach, salesperson, and human being.

It all starts with one revelation. Virtually every salesperson I talk to has the same story: They're fantastic at closing deals, but nobody can get any damn meetings.

As a client of mine, David, so eloquently put it:

"Before working with Justin, I STRUGGLED to book meetings. Now I'm booking meetings back-to-back and am the top rep across several teams - 100% recommend him (and he does seem to speak in tongues until you get to know him)."

I mentioned in the prologue that we're living in a world of noise. We're part of the digital era, one defined by endless babble in the form of sequencer cannons blasting inboxes, robocalls flooding phones, and pinging messenger notifications.

Flipping the script, breaking the pattern, and reworking communication, from prospecting, through to closing, is the only way to be heard.

I can tell you now that I've been in the exact same place as you are today. I've worked as a "commission only" seller, feeling like a replaceable cog in an ever-turning wheel. I've stared at my screen asking "how will I ever hit my target number?"

But I've also had a unique opportunity, to put on my lab coat, and start experimenting. That may be the only thing that differentiates me from you right now. I've tested the chemical reactions, and braved the explosions, to bring you something that works.

I've gone deeper into the A/B testing of methodologies than anyone I know, working closely with thousands of reps over the past seven years. I've experimented with strategies from making 40 cold calls in 40 days to one prospect, to using FaceTime Drops and sending custom Batman & Cinema Paradiso GIFs. I've convinced Nathan Offner to build me retro adventure video games starring my prospective customers with old-school gaming cartridges to complete the effect.

I've also sent every object thinkable via snail mail, sung songs and told jokes at the beginning of cold calls, and even sent poetry, haikus, and Justin Bieber lyrics in a desperate attempt to secure my dream prospect's attention.

On top of that, I've tested hundreds of tools, tech, and iterations of GPT prompts to reach the top of the proverbial mountain. I've found that, refreshingly, what I'm about to share applies very well to verticals like I.T., insurance, wealth management, real estate, pharma, consulting, coaching, and all professional services.

Like you, I've been inspired by the other innovators in my field and committed to researching their methods. However, I've also seen a genuine need for something new in this market. I wanted to create something that not only combines the insights I gained from my peers but builds on them.

What I hope to deliver here is an original approach to outbound sales that guides you to create your ideal sales method built from strategies that can continue to drive results long after hype cycles die out and economies change.

THE HUMAN MIND: THE FOUNDATION OF THE JMM

If there's one thing you need to know before you dive into the pages ahead it's this: the most powerful sales methodologies I've found are all built to respond to, leverage, and work with the human mind. Sales is a landscape built on relationships and communication. Both of these things are fundamentally human.

The reason I believe these methodologies work, and the reason why they've already earned endless positive testimonials from my clients is simple. These strategies are designed to resonate with the core foundations of what makes us human.

Sure, we're going to use AI and experiment with ChatGPT, automation, and technology along the way, but fundamentally, everything comes down to understanding how the brain works. The core workings of the human brain never change, no matter how much "neuroplasticity" you might have.

It doesn't matter your era, the unstable economy, tech stack limitations, or cultural background — I built this approach to work for everyone, even 100 years from now.

Why?

Because I'm not just teaching a strategy. I'm sharing a mindset, a modus operandi you can use throughout your sales career.

Hence, the iconic initial cover of the Justin Michael Method created by Milanese *Economist* magazine designer Luca D'Urbino, of the eternal sun rising from an envelope, symbolizing a new era of communication.

But to really master the "manipulation" of the human mind, you need to be willing to come with me through the entire journey. This means we're starting at the beginning.

As with any skill: you must first learn the basics before you begin to rewrite the rules. When you start to take those tentative steps toward achieving a goal, you've already overcome the biggest hurdle.

Unlike so many other sales professionals publishing their own books, I don't just want to tell you how to **close deals**. I want to show you how to cultivate opportunities, nurture them, and transform the entire pipeline.

First, we're going to get your mind in the right place. Then, we're going to explore how you can create abundance in your pipeline, using a holistic method. Too many sales methodologies lack any real insight into the first steps - prospecting, building rapport, and connecting with people.

In a world where generative AI is changing the face of sales and marketing, sales reps need a new way to stand out. I believe it's time to flip the script like Oren Klaff.

Better yet, burn the script and go full bore into "heuristics."

This method - your new outbound methodology - will teach you how to create a deep desire in any prospect for whatever you have to offer. It allows you to flip the polarity of the sales conversation, so it's their idea (never yours!) to not only take the meeting, but also embrace the deal.

How we open sales determines how we close: deal velocity, average contract value (ACV), and total contract value (TCV) on a multi-year basis. It even determines renewal potential. Oren Klaff calls this concept your "status frame."

First impressions count. In the crucible of those first nano-moments of an opening call lies the blueprint of an entire 7-figure deal. I believe that contract value is directly proportional to the quality of the first human interaction.

So, let's go back to the beginnings together, rework those foundations, and your ability to connect with the human mind. Let's channel your most human attributes, and unlock their full potential with new strategies and ideas.

Let's create a sales method that actually stands the test of time.

It's time to write it all down. We will go beyond the *Codices* and my previous books and guides. We will iron out the contradictions and build an 'Anarchist Cookbook' for good - a power user manual that will continue to serve others for decades to come.

It's time to start living up to your fullest potential. It's time to gain sales superpowers you never thought possible. I'll see you on the other side.

— *Justin Michael*

Los Angeles, California, USA
Stardate January 2nd, 2023
(43rd birthday, 22 years in sales)

Written to Ludovico Einaudi

Technical Editor's Note

Hi folks! My name is Greg Meyer - a long-time Justin fan and friend (we worked together at a past company and collaborated using many of these methods). My role here is to be your technical sherpa and help you surf the world of technical tools emerging in and around the sales space.

The most important tool you need to know is generative AI (Artificial Intelligence), a machine-learning model often powered by GPT (Generative Pre-Trained Transformer). Those are fancy words that you don't need to understand yet. My job is to break these concepts down for you in simpler terms so that you can apply them yourself. The critical thing to take away is that you can learn how to talk to computers and use them to improve almost anything.

You must also know what a Large Learning Model (LLM) means to understand how AI and GPT store information. An LLM is an advanced artificial intelligence program designed to understand and generate human-like text. It can learn patterns in language, interpret context, and produce responses based on the information it has been trained on.

An LLM is like a very sophisticated digital assistant that can read, write, and respond to text in a way that closely resembles how a human would.

At many points in this book, you'll see a sidebar called "GPT Lab:" we'll use this section to point out ways you can use GPT and AI tools to reinforce your learning and try things out. Keep in mind: there are no secret prompts. There is only the practice you gain by learning the best way to use this tech yourself!

- Greg Meyer

Bellingham, Washington, USA

Part I: JMM Genesis

"Coach Justin brought a power, insight and massive shortcuts into my world.

He saw things in me that I could not have seen myself and helped unlock completely new possibilities in business (and life) that I was blinded to by my own stories.

Remember that scene in The Matrix with Morpheus and Neo? It's like that.

The only way that works is to work with a GUIDE who has walked the path before at the highest levels of integrity. Justin knows the pitfalls and the possibilities on the path to massive revenue growth.

And his heart comes from a place of a true spirit of GIVING and a desire to help people see more in themselves than perhaps they see. Such is the nature of 'The Guide' and Justin is operating at the highest level for people and businesses.

Neo.

Obi Wan Kenobi.

Gandalf.

Justin Michael.

The end." – Brian Q Davis, EVP Scorpion

For the Record

"If you want to be successful in life, simply watch what most people would do in a given situation, and then do the total opposite—nine times out of ten, you'll receive greater rewards."

– Earl Nightingale

It's time to set the record straight.

Some of the stories I tell in this book might seem like self-validation. I often find the best way to teach is to start in a place of common ground. Sharing my stories with you is how I hope to convince you that we're more alike than we may appear.

In this book, I want to go beyond simply sharing my inventions and ideas. I want to show you clear, empirical evidence that these methods work. After all, if you're like most of the salespeople I meet, you're bound to be skeptical. We all are.

Despite years of experience in this industry, and a few successful books under my belt, I know I'm not coming to you from a place of power. I'm the guy telling you to restructure your whole mindset, rethink everything you've been taught and go back to the drawing board.

Some of the ideas you're going to encounter here will seem radical. You might ask yourself, if these methods are so effective, why they're not included in your company's sales training toolkit already?

The truth I've learned throughout my years in the sales industry is simple. Sometimes the "if it 'aint broke don't fix it" mentality just doesn't work. Some of us are so familiar with the same strategies that we use them over and over again without realizing how broken they actually are.

Sometimes we need to start fresh, throw out the rule book, and color outside of the lines.

If you're worried that your managers and supervisors won't approve these methods, tell them this. The strategies you're using might seem new and novel, but they're built on a simple concept: Neuroscience. The human brain is a puzzle to be unlocked, and that's exactly what we're going to do.

At the end of the day, we're all human beings with behaviors and defense mechanisms that are driven into us over time. Prospects lie to avoid difficult conversations or making decisions. Sellers desperately try to follow the crowd to avoid rocking the boat.

But imagine what would happen if, as a species, we didn't occasionally switch things up. What would have happened if we never looked for a form of travel beyond steam engines? Where would we be if we never asked what lay out there beyond the horizon, and propelled ourselves into the stars?

Innovation, and progress, both stem from change.

Now you might be wondering, "So what happens when everyone is using the JMM?" What's next when these methods become as commonplace as the cold selling techniques you already use every day? The answer is simple, we continue to innovate.

The methods you'll discover here are foundational building blocks, they create a structure you can continue to grow and develop for as long as you need to. Think of it like tilling the soil before a harvest, prepping it with the right fertilizer, and paving the way for growth.

It's ok if right now you see me as a radical. I've been labeled an outcast before. I was the first to build an outbound system where every message hit like a 'text message' or 'ad unit' and relied on visual prospecting as the payload in a 3-touch cluster. Before clusters, sellers sent emails like newsletters and drip marketing, day 1, 3, 5, 7, 11. They keep asking you to "take me off the list," because it looks so obvious that you put them on one!

I wasn't afraid to think outside of the box, and you shouldn't be either.

I encourage you to follow in my footsteps. Don't just be a salesperson. Be an inventor, a creator, and a dreamer. If I hadn't taken this approach, I never would have been the first person to prove to my team that frequency and saturation of touches are more important than even the context of an email.

I wouldn't have discovered that leaving 4-5 voicemails was necessary for success, even at a time when it was unheard of to reach out to prospects so frequently.

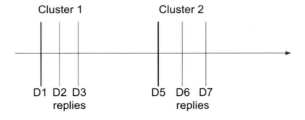

Email cluster visual of the sequence

I honestly believe outperforming your competitors, and standing out in the sales landscape sometimes means being a little bit of a maverick. Do what others are *not* doing. Otherwise how will you stand out?

I have probably been among the strongest proponents of parallel-assisted dialers (PADs). ConnectAndSell is the Ferrari of this space. The myth that holds people back is that you can't use it across a narrow total addressable market (TAM) or in Enterprise selling. Realistically, once you feed a PAD human-verified data, you're connecting live dozens of times on 1,000 dials per day. You start finishing the work of a five-person outbound SDR team in a quarter, in a matter of mere weeks.

Emailing one at a time is medieval at this point. Calling one phone number at a time is inefficient, and outdated.

> *"If I had asked people what they wanted, they would have said faster horses." – Henry Ford*

One point I want to note here is that this book, even with it's (slightly vain) name, doesn't just belong to me. I didn't create it on my own. Like you, I've had my tutors and mentors along the way. Shout out to Tony J. Hughes.

I've been his case study and collaborator over a decade. Like a Mandalorian apprentice, I learned the lost artform of selling with Tony as my Jedi knight.

Tony taught me how to *speak C-Level* and how to think about strategic sales because he led me to study the complete history of the craft. Check out *The Joshua Principle*, his superb first book, a parable to master strategic selling.

Of course, I've had plenty of great insights outside of Tony, too. I'm grateful for my first trainer at Salesforce, Todd Caponi (*The Transparency Sale*), who set me on good footing, and the precious time I've gotten to spend with the legendary Mike Bosworth, the Godfather of *Solution Selling*.

It's the guidance of these masters, windshield time with Eagles, combined with my own experience, research, and experimentation that led to the creation of this book. Most of the concepts I've covered here are painfully simple, but they're so frequently overlooked in the modern world.

Elon Musk and Tim Ferriss talk a great deal about deconstructing concepts to first principles and rebuilding them.

That idea has guided a lot of my thinking in this book, but it has also been a core part of my approach to life and sales in general. I'm not the next Tony Stark of B2B sales, with a level of superhero intellect. I'm just another person, like you, committed to learning, and growing.

The reality is that as human beings, we're programmed to question ourselves. But as salespeople, we should be questioning more.

Most of B2B sales is a lie. Question everything, Neo.

As you progress through the pages here, I hope they inspire you to ask, "why?" I want you to take a hard look at your cold calling method and ask yourself *why* you still open calls with clichéd permission-based openers (PBOs) from 2010 like, "Did I catch you at a bad time?" That immediately lowers your status in the eyes of your prospect.

Why would you cold pitch an emotional homo sapiens with logic like "the reason for my call is..." when we know we've triggered 'fight or flight' and only actively listening can calm them down to control the call? Wouldn't we want to lower our prospect's resistance by displaying emotional intelligence (EQ), empathy and understanding?

> *"I too hate PBOs. CXOs don't ask permission. You have to act like one." – Moeed Amin*

Don't follow a strategy just because it's popular on LinkedIn. Ask, does it really work, or are you just stuck on repeat? What is popular is already not working because everyone is doing it.

I want you to ask yourself *why* you send an abundance of words to prospects in emails, rather than filling their imagination with vivid *images*. Why do you handle objections with combativeness, rather than validation and working with the fear, social-Aikido style? *Why* do you continue to "pitch slap" on LinkedIn, rather than building rapport via real-time chat.

In simple terms, start asking: "Why?" Even: "What if?"

People, despite their wisdom, are often 'sheeple.' Following the crowd might make you popular in high school, but it's not how you win at life. Success is a long game, there are no "get rich quick" fixes. If 999 sellers do it the same, and you do the opposite, you're the one that stands out. Zig while they zag.

I'm not sure why nobody since David Sandler had come along to question and reimagine everything in B2B sales. I think the empirical approach to innovation is uncomfortable, even scary. People fundamentally fear change. It takes courage, bravery, experimentation and a thick skin.

When you bring something new to the world, there's always someone lining up to question you with a vested interest in the old way. Sometimes, they'll try to discredit, and disprove you too.

I've had companies that raised hundreds of millions deliberately release case studies to disprove the "thoughts?" bump for example. But I receive screenshots daily to prove it still works like a charm.

There will always be haters. But everything you've read in this book is included here because it works. I've built this book around ideas infused with human psychology and heuristics (mental shortcuts), not tactics.

What you may not realize, is I'm not the only proponent of thinking outside of the box. I'm just being more direct with my suggestions.

Jeremey Donovan, SVP of Revenue Strategy at Salesloft at the time, tested many similar hypotheses on 6MM anonymized emails. My empirical experiments blowing millions (responsibly?) in angel investor capital, matched nearly identically.

I've validated these methods, then built on them, expanding into the new era, and the new world, where OpenAI and generative AI intelligence is beginning to change the landscape. The technology might evolve, but the principles won't.

> *"I saw the angel in the marble and carved until I set him free." – Michelangelo*

Even if ChatGPT and similar tools do change sales forever, it's still us, the humans that shape the bots. Our methodologies, strategies, and belief systems determine what we get out of our robotic companions.

Even if machines pass the Turing Test, we will still work with them like the lathe of God, to fine tune and calibrate their endless iteration in cascading arcs, and upward spirals of sophistication.

Everything in the JMM is meta

> *"Justin is at the cutting edge of what's possible with the semi-automation happening in B2B sales. His commitment to sharing his knowledge is outstanding. He also has a knack for bringing together the best practices resident in the minds of the top sales thinkers worldwide. Additionally, Justin helped our team redesign our cadences/sequences with solid improvements. I highly recommend that everyone follow JM and engage his company when they need fresh approaches."*
>
> *– SVP, Sales Excellence at Mediafly*

The JMM is a formula or framework sitting on top of the linguistics that governs effective communication, never a template. Some elements to display acumen are like Bob Ross's "paint by numbers." I deliberately write display as there's often no time to learn in ramping up new reps.

With the techniques in this book, you can take a 22-year-old student straight out of Uni and make them sound like a seasoned 20-year veteran at sales. Acumen development is the whole goal. By asking better questions, you sound more savvy. Like that famous Dale Carnegie story where the job interviewer talks the whole time and then exclaims, "you're the best conversationalist ever in my office."

Every human you meet is a distinct and profound learning opportunity. So be open to an ever-evolving education.

Learn from prospects on every call, and remember, learning can be fun.

I collected baseball cards very avidly as a kid, studied all the stats, knew every card/player in every pack and box set. In my mid-30s after almost burning out in outbound sales, I realized I could become obsessed by turning hunting prospects into a game. Instead of cards, I'd collect people's life stories.

To illustrate my point, on every call you have this week, ask your prospect:

- How does your company monetize?
- What's your business model?
- What are your KPIs, application programming interfaces (APIs), and channels?
- What's unique about your technology?
- How do you (personally) make money?
- What's the background of your people and company that made you scale?
- Are you private or public (and why); how do your deals work to get capitalized or funded?
- Who are your VCs and why did they invest (where else did the VC firm invest)?

Learn all day and get stronger while others complain and slog. Acumen is the byproduct of sheer curiosity.

"Want to become an expert in business?" A millionaire once asked me. Read the obituaries. I know that sounds morbid but successful people leave clues as to their success and the myriad ways in which you can build a business are awe-inspiring. There are 400MM small businesses worldwide.

Dovetail that fact with the 40% of workers that side hustle, and you'll want to definitely consider creating a supplemental income now, not later (5-20K/mo.), even if you're killing it. (*See my chapter on Side Hustles in Part VIII*)

Why am I the first person to see all this and codify it?

I'd like to tell you that I'm some sort of genius, reassure you with grandiose tales of my incredible IQ. I'm proud to say I have accomplished a great deal in my life. But I've also struggled. I'm the progeny of a linguistics Ph.D. who spoke fluent Mandarin and the grandson of a nuclear physicist who ran a particle accelerator.

Yet despite this, I left school at 15 (tested out), managed, produced and marketed musicians, and never really went anywhere in my twenties. I fell into sales in 2001 and eventually made it to Salesforce and LinkedIn in the 2010s by sheer "pig-headed discipline and determination" (hat tip Chet Holmes) to sell the next generation of marketing automation software, even after they rejected me countless times.

The reality is that anyone can be exceptional. Anyone can look beyond the curtain, if they choose to do so. Bill Gates lived in Seattle in the days when you could rent punch cards to code primitively into mainframes. Steve Jobs interned for Hewlett-Packard in his teens after successfully cold-calling Bill Hewlett. I love that story! Right place, right time, so they say.

I've "felt the fear" and did it anyway. Curiosity and experimentation go hand-in-hand. Embracing both lets you see things from a new perspective.

I worked in mobile technology for nearly two decades and realized the messages we were all sending via smartphones to generate new business needed to be fixed. Cornerstone insights hit me like a ton of bricks when I sent a Venn Diagram to the Chief Digital Officer of McDonald's and set a meeting on the first try.

Then the VP of Mobile at Home Depot called me from my email signature and said, "I got your diagram; pitch me." Talk about my Flux Capacitor moment slipping on a toilet, hitting my head, and inventing time travel. Smartphones may even be gone by the time you read this, but the heuristics principles herein will remain just as effective. Even if you're programming your open-source AIs to implement it.

I developed my signature phone opener, Route-Ruin-Multiply (RRM), also modified to Route-Ruin-Rip (RRR), at 27, selling SaaS fundraising software to executive directors in nonprofits. I A/B tested thousands of phone openers and multi-threading paths to find this "Jedi mind trick." This was the first time anyone had leveraged Pareto in the first 10 seconds, with the customer doing most of the talking.

In 2022, I found a wrinkle in how to build DM chat threads, a framework for interaction that flips polarity similar to the RUIN step of RRM (reach out for Codex 7 and 13). It's called "The 4th Frame" and we'll explore it from every possible angle later in the book.

You could call all of this "luck" or "good fortune," and I suppose you're partially right. But unlike luck, your growth as a salesperson is something you can control. What I hope to do here is give you the power and confidence to make the first move.

That means I'm going beyond the basics covered in my previous volumes. I'm diving into the information I usually reserve for pay-ing coaching clients, to "spread the love" to those who need it most. All I ask in return is that you invest in yourself.

Feel the curiosity, embrace the change. Do something new.

I taught this 4th Frame real-time chat flow technique to a branding expert in his twenties. He opened 80K in pipeline in the first 72 hours. I taught a rep this at Salesforce. He quit his job and was ROI positive on his investment into my 1:1 coaching within 3 weeks. Now he's quit AE life to go full time on coaching and is traveling the world already replacing his SaaS income. What a champion!

Results define our work and the efficacy of any methodology. After grinding on the JMM for twenty years, I've coached thousands of sellers and startups to apply it, developing these ideas even further through application and A/B testing.

Just as these techniques helped me to raise myself up from commission-only inside sales to one of the highest-paid VPs ever in SaaS, they can do the same for you.

As a salesperson you're taught never to give anything away for free. Everything has a price, they say. So, why am I sharing all this? The simple answer is that I believe in generosity. I'll tell you multiple times in this book you need to be a "giver" not a "taker" to succeed in sales.

The evidence that these methodologies do make a difference is overwhelming. I'm constantly receiving testimonials from people I've shared the same insights with. Paul hit President's club and was promoted twice in 7 months. Kelvin hit 190% quota by applying the *Codex Guides* to a new SDR function he built from scratch. (All *Codices* are open source and freely available at this link, just log in and click exclusive content: hypcccycl.com/codexes). Pat went from a garbage truck to owning his own home in Seattle.

So yes, this method truly works.

But once again, you need to be willing to jump in and approach all this with the right mindset. I can tell you I've helped executives triple their pipelines and leave the rat race entirely until the cows come home, but it's up to you to take the plunge.

I hope, by sharing my own stories, I can inspire you to see yourself in me, and envision the success you can bring your way.

I lived check to check and fell into sales, and despite a flash of brilliance at 21 in 2001 telemarketing and managing/supervising call centers, I didn't have much belief in my ability. I'd never read a single sales book or been coached or mentored the first ten years. It was painful, miserable, and really just a day job for me.

I despised going to a restaurant or club and couldn't even afford a drink. I was embarrassed to admit to my friends I was out of a job. Recruiters were telling me to lie and say "some college" on my resume. I even risked my life (bodyguard in tow) managing call centers in San José, Costa Rica.

Disillusioned, I followed the techno Gold Rush North to SF and interviewed for a few months with 2K to my name.

I was about to give up hope when visualization techniques to music I developed (request a hidden paper called Musifestation) led to me being hired by Sean Parker (Co-Founder of Facebook-Meta, youngest billionaire in the world at the time) and jumping immediately to over 100K in income. Through a positive mindset and a hell of a lot of hard work, I networked my way to Salesforce the following year.

But it was only by 35 (after nearly 15 years of experience) that I took matters into my own hands to build out my own methodology. I broke 250K base, then earned over 500K, then over 1MM applying all the methods I've shown you in this book.

I went from an average, bag-carrying sales rep at Salesforce, to a top VP of SaaS for mobile companies you've probably never heard of closing 3MM on a 1.25MM quota in my last banner year before I retired from SaaS field sales altogether *to coach you*.

So let's take the next step in our respective journeys together. Let's break the molds and break free from restrictive comfort zones. It's time to evolve.

A METHOD TO MY MADNESS

Revolutionary tombstone realizations that challenge everything:

The JMM Core Axioms:

1. Email is visual - not templates
2. Cold calling is about power transfer - not scripts and tone
3. One cold call 'live' connect – aka "complete" – is equivalent to multiple DM chats back and forth (see the 4th frame)

If you're not having real one-to-one conversations with other humans every day in any medium, it's not "sales." The silent sales floor is killing businesses, per Tony J. Hughes – clicking, liking, tweeting, and Tik Toking your brains out is probably just *marketing*.

So ask yourself one question: Are you a marketing analyst or a sales leader? "Justin, this coaching doesn't apply to me, I'm not a sales leader." I get this feedback a lot when I reach out. "Oh but you are, you are a leader. Great selling *is leadership* no matter what level you're at on the corporate food chain."

I worked in the shadows for two decades. It wasn't until 2020 that I started to shine a light on myself, for the sole purpose of shattering the prevailing paradigm of 10,000+ books, methods, and dark guru consultants, but there are a select few methodologies I truly respect that have withstood the test of time, e.g. SPIN, Target

Account Selling (TAS), Challenger, Sandler, Power Base Selling, Diagnostic Business Development, Solution Selling, and Miller Heiman. Couldn't I bring this level of rigor to TOFU: top of the funnel?

B2B is like a big high school or 'Best in Show.' People focus on fame and money, seldom ever making a real impact. Those who can't do, teach. I still cold call and work every last tactic in this book to the bone including testing many on the gray hat edge until they are safe to use. I have no interest in the juvenile game of "who has the best purebred poodle." Nope, I didn't make it to the Top Sales Leader List but last time I checked, that doesn't measure impact, service to humanity, or your bank account. You can't take it with you; there's no luggage rack in heaven.

Here's how wealth and success really work:

More service = more prosperity

The more you serve your customers/clients, the more money you make. The more abundance and prosperity flow to you.

Hence, I'm on a mission to elevate the sales profession and help everyone who reads my work succeed more today. If you apply what I write here verbatim you'll see immediate improvement as all systems are perfectly dictated by their inputs.

GIGO: Garbage in garbage out.

The problem is people are addicted to the drama. We need to move from a victim to an owner mentality to fix our self esteem through excellence in execution. I'm not discounting the power of therapy but I'm here to coach you, right? If I didn't get my clients massive results, they would never renew.

That's the beauty of this profession and the litmus test which is transference of success principles translating into new outcomes in a virtuous cycle. Ironically, we are all our own worst enemy self sabotaging our personal growth. Why? Hedonic adaptation.

"You can never get enough of what you DON'T need to make you happy." - Eric Hoffer

Example: I've grown my following to over 50,000 on LinkedIn and capped out my 30,000 direct connections. I'm pigeonholed as one of the top 5 sales development / prospecting minds globally, (and finally got acknowledged as a LinkedIn Top Sales Voice), yet I coach/train executives on *full-cycle* sales approaches at all skill levels.

Do the accolades land me clients? Nope, conversations that create real relationships do. Period.

My nicknames in the field were "hummingbird," "honey badger," and "the machine." Eventually, I earned the name: "Salesborg" or just "Borg." I became "Salesborg," seller meets cyborg, by doing what I encouraged you to do in *Tech-Powered Sales* (TPS) - up-skilling your technology quotient (TQ) and testing every possible software you can get your hands on. But I found I lost my soul and effectiveness seeking to fully automate everything.

To sell is human.

All my best results came when I slowed down and focused, work-ing with one human at a time. And now I'm here to help you slow down so that a brand new world of sales can open up for you as it has for me and so many I've coached. A brilliant new horizon line of ability will stretch out as far as the eye can see, and a new day will dawn on your results. You can and *will* shatter your own income ceiling and self-imposed limitations.

At this writing, I'm very deep into OpenAI's GPT which could surpass version GPT-10 by the time you read this, maybe even further. We're going to cover this technology a lot during this book, but don't worry.

This is not the tech stack book, this is *the method behind it.* I want you to use this book to exceed my success by becoming some mutant combination of all of the above: a digital honey badger, hummingbird-cyborg-sales-bot (but in the best way!)

I'm laser-focused on one thing after raising myself up from 5 figures to 7: **doubling and tripling your pipeline, commission, and income.**

Countless positive testimonials have shown me this should be the focus of my coaching practice. 10 million technology sellers suffer from consistent growth problems, even if they don't admit it to themselves. I want to show you how I cracked that code, so you can do it too.

I've said it before and I'll say it again. This book isn't about me. It's about you. What you learned today is going to make you so confident in your ability to create new business that if you were dropped into any country from a helicopter with nothing but a loincloth, you'd still be able to build a 6-7 figure empire within months.

There is no easy button. But right *being*, right *thinking*, and right *actions* lead to precise outcomes. If you're willing to put in the reps and suffer through unnatural elements, unlearning sales (*Codex 17*), you will succeed wildly.

GPT Lab: Unlearning what you've learned

Uncover your unconscious bias. Ask GPT to ask you your assumptions about sales.

Here's a prompt to help you with this:

"Imagine you are a salesperson who has been given the task of selling a new product to a potential customer. The customer is initially hesitant about the product, and expresses concerns about its price and functionality. How would you address these concerns and persuade the customer to make the purchase? Be specific in your approach, and explain why you believe it would be effective."

PART II: THE JMM MINDSET

Who we are 'being' influences our 'thinking' and ultimately controls our 'doing.'

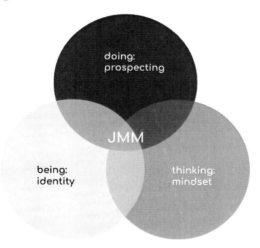

JMM Mindset Venn Diagram

Remember that. It's our dharma or "essential nature" — an apple seed cannot grow into an orange tree. If we are consistently "struggling to succeed" and tell ourselves: "I'm *trying* to earn seven figures," we will attract a constant state of "struggling" and "trying" rather than simply "doing."

When you *are* a top performer, your mindset and daily affirmations sound different, like, "I *am* triumphantly and easily earning seven figures by serving my ideal customers transformationally."

Can you see that distinction?

Eliminate the word *trying* as Yoda did, "Try not, do." Endless *trying* infects the speech of so many executives - it dooms you to a life like Sisyphus, endlessly pushing a boulder up the mountain of another quarterly milestone missed.

Guard your speech because it will harden into fact and reality. Be, do, and live - never try. All success in life is going to hinge on action.

From right thought, right action springs eternal.

This book isn't a guide to arrogant living. It's an instruction manual for how you can take control of your thoughts, actions, and processes to achieve more.

Live by the 3Ps: Patience, Persistence, and Perspicacity. Perspicacity means "keenness in discernment," translation: "constant vigilance."

The idea is to remain an empirical skeptic and practice *pronoia*. In other words, believe the universe isn't out to get you–rather, it's constantly finding new ways to present opportunities. You just need to know how to see, and grasp those opportunities, when they arise.

It's cultivating the right mindset, processes, and approach to life that will make you more effective in sales. I'm here to tell you how to create a new identity that helps you to thrive in your role, whatever that might be.

After all, our identity controls what we become.

A 200K mindset can't yield consistent 500K earnings, just like a chain smoker can't *try out* non-smoking and expect to sustain results quickly.

So...

Let's start with your outlook

Miyamoto Musashi said it best:

> *"There is nothing outside of yourself that can ever enable you to get better, stronger, richer, quicker, or smarter. Everything is within. Everything exists. Seek nothing outside of yourself."*

Everything starts with mindset.

Start by shifting yourself from a fixed mindset to a growth mindset. A salesperson with a fixed mindset locks themselves into the same repeating pattern because they don't believe they can change.

A growth mindset shifts your focus from 'what you cannot do' to 'what you cannot do *yet*.' The 'yet' is crucial.

You go from "cannot" to "can-do" only by *doing*.

The power is in *doing* (more so in sales than in any other role you can imagine).

Approach your study with a white belt mindset, and remember my earlier injunction: "There's nothing I do that you cannot." I'm just an average Joe that made good on his life. I learned the knowledge shared in this book through trial and error; painful lessons and satisfying victories.

Approach what you're about to read with an open mind and an adventurous spirit. Tremendous rigor and respect for the scientific method went into discovering and codifying this material, so there isn't anything left to chance.

This method works because it rests on a logical progression: by *thinking* in a new way, in heuristics, in shortcuts, and in formulas, the things you *do* – aka templates, scripts, and sequences – will evolve too.

Follow this method as precisely as you can and watch your new business pipeline explode. Within a little practice, you will become a 3rd-degree black belt in customer acquisition.

Let me tell you a little secret. It's easier than you think. Not because the concepts you are going to practice are not going to take mental fortitude and persistence, but because simply *trying* is half the battle.

Outbound sellers have sold the same broken way for the last 100 years; most will continue to do so. Only the top 1% change with time and set the new rules of the game.

We'll approach that broken way anew through the lens of armchair neuroscience, poke holes in it, pull it apart, reconstruct it and discover what it means to be the rare executive who stands out in a crowd.

The 1%.

You will notice changes soon after you adopt the ideas in this book to your daily life. Like going to the gym to get that beach body, consistency is key.

While the tiny shifts to your strategy may seem subtle at first, layered on top of each other, these changes will make a noticeable difference. Cumulatively you'll develop a whole new pattern that sends a signal to your prospects: You are unique. You are someone they want to work with. You are someone that has earned their time and attention.

You have probably heard the phrase, 'opening is the new closing.' I think I first heard it from Anthony Iannarino. This book teaches you how to 'open' new business and lead people to the promised land of your solution. It will rapidly and unconsciously become "their idea" to take the meeting. And you'll know exactly *why*.

These are the outbound operating principles that <u>work</u>.

Tell yourself that you're on the right path. Stop letting the fear of change keep you paralyzed and immobile. Train your mind for curiosity, creativity, and tenacity, and the rest will come naturally.

Honey Badger Don't Care

Be fearless and consistent, like the honey badger.

Let me tell you a story...

My friend Pat owed a credit card company 15 Gs. Every day, he got the same call: "Patrick, this is Joe Maricelli, call me back." Literally every day, the same call, like clockwork, 50 days in a row. Finally, I got curious. I picked up the phone and decided to handle the issue for him.

I said, "Joe, Patrick is never going to pay this bill. But if you'll settle for two thousand dollars right now, he's open to it."

Response: "Sure, what's your card number?"

People rarely handle their credit card bills - at least not without a fight. So, of course, Joe was happy to win any sum of money - even if it wasn't the amount he was originally hoping for.

But, what earned Joe that win? Was it constantly trying to negotiate and sweet talk? Nope. It was endurance. Joe never lost his cool, or his determination. He kept calling until he broke through.

As a sales professional, this got me thinking. "What if I go full Joe Maricelli?" What if I turn the dial up a notch - almost to stalking levels - but elegantly?

Going "ham" with my emails didn't lead to restraining orders, surprisingly enough. It actually helped me to win more deals. It made me more compelling, more interesting, and more successful. It can do the same for you.

I have had a lot of CXOs call me back and try to hire me or ask to train their people, based just on my approach to persistence. True story.

As Kraig Kleeman loves to say, they "must react." The prospects are spiders in the drain; if you turn the spigot all the way up, they just hide out and crawl back up. But if you turn on a fire hose of persistent insight, they're forced to respond.

Of course, there is a finesse to this strategy.

Don't forget to put the honey in the stately honey badger.

Honey badgers are astoundingly resilient. They're known for tackling animals much larger than themselves. They're immune to cobra venom, and barely flinch when they're spiked with porcupine quills. Heck, they can even frighten off some of nature's biggest threats like a pride of lions. Doesn't this sound like "prospecting" in the 2020s and beyond?

I look at the honey badger as the unofficial mascot of the sales landscape. But there are other creatures who also show some of the characteristics sales leaders need to master.

Let's look at the Great White Shark for instance. These marvels are endurance professionals. They keep swimming, even when they're asleep. When they eat a seal, they breach the ocean's surface fully. Imagine the raw power required for this apex predator to swim that hard.

As a hat tip to Craig Simons at Allego, I'll throw in orcas and wolves as worthy mascots too. They work in teams. Give this book to another executive and co-sell or if you're in the same org, split commission on some whale-hunting deals while you synergize your application of these ideas.

Metaphors abound in our attitudes to selling to the powerful. (I wrote about this at length in *Codex 16* - "Phonistry," happy to share it with you directly.)

Burn the Ships

If you had 30 days to live, would you bank on yourself or Some Random Company, Inc? I rest my case. Why not go all in on the "startup of you" (Reid Hoffman) to maximize your earning potential? Launch that side hustle now. Go into business for yourself. The time is now. No more excuses.

"Twenty years from now you will be more disappointed by the things you didn't do than by the ones you did do. So throw off the bowlines! Sail away from safe harbor. Catch the trade winds in your sails. Explore. Dream. Discover!" – Mark Twain

> *If I could do it as a high school dropout that worked my way up to Salesforce and LinkedIn even after being rejected hundreds of times, you can too.*

Think you're not destined for greatness? Neither did I.

It took me 20 years to become a "success" despite being the grandson of an august nuclear physicist that knew Richard Feynman and the brother of a Google-level engineer who aced the Ivy League at Computer Science.

My mantra: We can't die with our music still inside us (Maslow-Dyer), and many of us plateau our entire lives in quiet desperation waiting to live up to our unlimited potential.

Part of the problem is an unequivocal need for speed. We all want things to happen now - or even better, yesterday. We're impatient in virtually every aspect of our lives. Just look at how many people have replaced reading books with watching snippets and reviews on YouTube.

Slow down to speed up. Slowly ingest this book, read it 5 times. My new mascot is a snail. Let's be happy, patient little garden snails. You'd never expect to hear that from that random, terminator-faced cyborg guy you saw on LinkedIn but soon you'll understand exactly *why*.

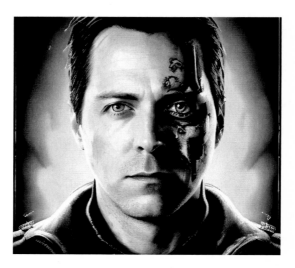

Image created with Stable Diffusion, an open-source
AI deep learning model.

Be yourself; everyone else is taken. When I first photoshopped that android on my face, a very famous thought leader wrote me on LinkedIn to warn me, "that's a career-limiting move" (CLM). Then my book "TPS" hit the top 20 on Amazon/Audible and held there for 2 years, thanks to so many of you reading this now. I got blacklisted to a degree in the industry but after 4 years of crusading for a top funnel revolution, some of the biggest detractors are now on a real-time chat basis and referring me major clients.

"First they ignore you, then they laugh at you, then they fight you, then you win." – Gandhi

Decide now. Do you want to build your business on commerce or service? This book is about the service-based route. Not inbound, not "scaling with courses."

Wake up. Visit with good people. Transform their lives. Rinse and repeat. Always fewer clients. Better quality clients. Deeper relationships

Less is more. More with less. Live The Pareto Principle.

Many people I work with suffer from imposter syndrome even in the most senior SVP and CEO positions. While I'm not a psychotherapist and can't change your childhood trauma, I can arm you with effective techniques that immediately start to work in the market – today. As you begin to succeed, this growing "market validation," as David C. Baker calls it, gives you renewed confidence and builds upon itself.

Within 90 days of practicing this method, self-esteem turns around and jumps like a flickering blue ember into an unquenchable Olympic flame, and your courage becomes unstoppable.

"Courage is rightly esteemed the first of human qualities because it has been said, it is the quality which guarantees all others." – Winston Churchill

Admittedly, I'm biased. I created this book after setting world records for outbound prospecting and top-funnel creation wherever I went, working for 13 technology ventures as a hunter, individual contributor (IC) or player-coach Vice President (VP).

Do I seem like I lack humility? I know who I am, my strengths and limitations. Everyone told me *Tech-Powered Sales* was too complex, nearly impossible to read like a "defense contractor manual," but I poured myself into it authentically and my niche found me, those hundred true fans became 1,000, then 10,000, and now 10s of thousands. My entire life is dedicated to serving one potential client at a time: **you, reading this work now**, however it got to you.

> *"If there's resistance, self interest is getting in the way or fear. You're not in service, you're not enjoying it." — John Patrick Morgan*

This book isn't about my legacy, it's about creating yours. Building a new future starts with breaking things down, rethinking the fundamentals, and adding your own spin.

So many people copied David Sandler, he's the Paul McCartney of sales.

My thesis is: why can't anyone be the next Sandler?

Why can't you take this book and cultivate a new life for yourself?

GPT Lab: Use GPT to think differently

GPT is a clever tool to ask yourself if you are thinking divergently.

After a question, use a follow-on prompt like "Help me understand if this is a conventional way to understand [insert the problem you are discussing here]. What am I missing?"

Sell Around The Curve (Future Visioning)

Holistic thinking and future visioning transform the sales journey.

Customers are rarely blown away by your core offering. Listing features or opportunities 101-style doesn't work. You need to play up to their intelligence with 202 and 303 content. Introduce the *art of the possible.*

Don't be "SaaS for Dummies."

Nobody understands this strategy better than Marc Benioff, Salesforce CEO (ever notice that safe harbor warning every Dreamforce presentation?)

I used to sell mobile marketing automation technology and this is what it actually looked like:

- Sell around the curve (we opened sales convos focused on personalized push notifications & omnichannel orchestration)
- Close down hill into the core (they ultimately bought basic push notifications)
- Sell to Innovators & Early Adopters (16% of any market according to Geoffrey Moore's curve)

In the words of Gary Littlefair, "Deals often close on one use case." Keep this in mind when doing *use-case selling*, a trojan horse in Enterprise.

In short: Sell the future vision road map features - close on your core product offering.

Imagine you're working with a client that's selling self-piloting drones for high voltage power plant sites. So, how do you present the unique value proposition?

Ask your prospect to imagine something:

Imagine if you didn't have to send humans in bucket trucks. Now imagine if you didn't need to send humans at all. Just install the drone substation boxes, the drones self-deploy, fly around monitoring dangerous, million voltage grids and go back to the box autonomously.

Tech like this is still being developed, but if you can create that vision, and imagine that future with your prospect, you capture the mind of the decision maker. You encourage them to "see around the curve."

Sell around the curve, close on the core. This is the great secret to attracting the fastest SaaS sales cycles.

Another technique I respect comes from Townsend Wardlaw: Referential Value Proposition.

"I don't talk about what I do or do for people. I talk about how my services have served others like the individual I'm reaching out to in their words, in their language. What's the problem on their mind?

Example: I serve founders of 2-10MM companies like yourself who are stuck somewhere on the journey and are getting frustrated by the fact they have to do everything themselves despite hiring people."

"Don't sell what you do. Don't sell what you do for them. Sell what you do for them, does for them!" – T.W.

Charles Manning is the CEO of Kochava, former Oracle product visionary, and one of the top CEOs I respect in tech. He also writes blogs and whitepapers about blockchain and AI revolutionizing all AdTech that are the 202 and 303 level "most advanced" content I've ever seen in the space. I admired his content from afar and got to know him personally - he's a humble genius.

His eloquence attracts the CEOs of Fortune 500 companies consistently so I'm not surprised many are his clients.

When I sold enterprise software, I took this tack. Not the 101 or "AdTech for Dummies" style where you talk down to your prospects like children. I put out sophisticated posts, interacted with top analysts, gave cryptic opinions, and punched above my weight on the technology. This brought the elite buyers my way. They thought, "JM is an expert on mobile software development kits (SDKs) and attribution."

What blew my mind is that I attracted a 9-step interview cycle as a mobile product manager for a company so famous I can't mention it. In all due humility, I was the least technical person in sales when I started. But as my colleague Itai Kafri used to say, "Justin is technically curious." My hunger to question, to ask, to be curious, to deep dive with sales engineers and our CTO, made me stand out. I tried with all my might to master the tech and be more "in tune" with the stack. That meant often researching beyond the information given to us in our documentation.

I just spoke with the Co-Founder of Sybill, Nishit Asnani, and he still credits the "future of selling" section in *Tech-Powered Sales* as being a core inspiration of what he's building toward in the product roadmap. How can you apply this?

1. Read the blogs from the top analysts in your space
2. Read books like *Machine Platform Crowd* (Andrew McAfee, Erik Brynjolfsson) about the future of AI
3. Be ahead of the curve learning the advanced applications of ChatGPT and OpenAI prompt engineering
4. Network with founders like Karan Korpal Sharma who understand where technology is going for GTM
5. Get into futuristic conversations with your prospects
6. Paint a picture of your most involved, most advanced, use case of your platform - positioned as a comprehensive platform solution not just a "point solution" or one-trick pony

Sell the future. Close on the core.

GPT Lab: Skate to where the puck is going

GPT can help you think about potential future outcomes, even if it can't predict the future.

One way to think about this is to build prompts that help you think about challenges in short (a few days or months), medium (6-12 months), and long-term time frames (2+ years):

"Help me build a prompt to encourage thinking along different time frames. I want you to help me consider challenges and opportunities in short (a few days or months), medium (6-12 months), and long-term time frames (2+ years) - including in the prompt the ability to ask me what question I want to consider. Wait to write out the whole prompt until you have asked me the question and I have answered, then submit the prompt as if I have asked you that prompt."

PART III: COACHING AND GROWTH

"What you think you become, what you feel you attract, what you imagine you create."

– Buddha

FIRST PRINCIPLES

"You are a razor with many blades which are your diversified income streams."

– Marylou Tyler

"The more enigmatic, the higher the fee."

– Bryan Franklin

A potential recruiter client in Dubai told me, "Justin, I *don't* need help with my mindset." "OK," I replied, "How much are you earning?" "200K." "That won't get you very far in Dubai," I joked.

Sarcasm aside, the way to double your success starts with who you're *being*, before *thinking*, and *doing*. The greatest coaches approach their clients from the inside out. It's always an inner game to shift your identity if you look at it like *Atomic Habits* by James Clear or Cal Newport's superb book riffing on the Steve Martin quote, "be so good they can't ignore you."

Agreeing with that logic, he immediately signed up for my coaching and has been an absolute champion smashing it with the JMM.

It's a big deal when you make your first 100K in one day; it feels euphoric. 200K is more subtle. But when you do your first 100K or 200K commission day, or 500K to 1MM+ year, there are no words to describe the true triumph you'll experience. Taxes sting, my friend. I call this "a quality problem."

My interpretation of what psychologists refer to as the 'hedonic treadmill' and 'hedonic adaptation' is that we tend to always create the comfort zone of (un)happiness and prosperity (or lack thereof) we are accustomed to. Hedonism tells us: To live for pleasure, lavish expenditure, to seek pleasure in things. But the best things in life aren't things – *still*.

That's why lottery winners are so often bankrupt within mere years of winning outrageous sums of cash. That's why million dollar earners spend 1.3MM and go into debt keeping up with the Joneses.

While trying to break your income ceiling you still hold it in place subconsciously. Realizing this – maybe even now reading this book – is the first step to shattering it.

I've been there, done that, and got the t-shirt. I've walked that road, the same one you're on now. It's the fact that we've all had these experiences that convinces me this book will continue to have value, even when I'm dead and gone.

I find it amusing when 7-figure earners in the right company at the right place and time advise on serendipity. Or they claim, 'I have a dozen friends that made seven figures.' If those are your odds, run.

No matter how stuck you feel reading this, I assure you that you can double or triple your income rapidly. Especially if you're in the wrong company and a messed-up life situation. Nobody got it more wrong than me to bounce back from near death and get it right.

I never thought I'd publish books, train thousands of reps, or advise hundreds of startups. I wasn't convinced I'd live until 30 or hold down a job. I almost called my method *Political Selling* because I was such a victim of them but politics are wildly unpopular, the proverbial "third rail." Strange: *90% of moving up in tech companies is about politics and optics. Not how good you are at selling.* It's a paradox.

Politics drive customers to buy - it's either fame/power or money and many leaders especially in I.T. and Marketing aren't incentivized by money; they want to look good in front of their boss, so they get promoted or receive accolades. Making your customers heroes so they get promoted is a faster driver of making sales than just about anything you can read in a sales book.

I work with many high performers. Because once I became one, I was suddenly a victim of my own success. I kept self sabotaging my ability to advise, consult, side hustle and break free from my 9-to-5 with some bizarre loyalty to "the Man" and corporate exclusivity.

Nobody wins when you put driving 10s of millions in revenue to a faceless corporation over building generational wealth for your own family. Trust me. But there are some phenomenal ventures where taking 1-3 percentage points of equity on the deal as an early VP is well worth it. Or, the culture and leadership is so good, sticking there for a tour of duty of 2-4 years, can be worth a master's degree or PhD in "real-world" experience. Can't say enough good things about LinkedIn and Salesforce for that.

I have lived the concept of exponential growth. You put in the hard work on the road toward mastery, hitting one plateau after another, and suddenly there's a rapid spike, and you break through. Every competent seller understands this hockeystick of ability, having reached the level they're at.

I remember my first discovery calls, pacing, and heavy breathing at Salesforce. I had no idea how to run a client call. Now I find each call as relaxing as lazing on the beach. It all started with changing my mindset, and taking a new approach.

Repetition is the mother of skill and we build out an unconscious competence as we drill, rehearse, and role play. Want to become the best in your industry? Repetition or "reps," as Garrett "GMAC" MacDonald would say.

I got the rare privilege in 2017/18 to backfill a co-founder and run Ops in a special project to create an AI model of my brain, spending $3MM in VC on A/B tests from 100+ sequencer instances, 400+ Gmail accounts, engineering team of 17 in tow, and scaling to 100 concurrent customers toward a 10MM ARR. The same patterns emerged with B2B Comms (communications) over and over again and nobody is talking about them. *Still.*

That's why my favorite messages to get are, "I was doing this back at Oracle in 2005," or, "I always knew this but nobody has ever articulated it before until you came along."

The JMM system is gravity for B2B Sales. It's Newtonian. No matter where you drop an apple on Earth, it still falls in exactly the same way.

Initially, I built this resource for high-end coaching clients. I wasn't going to release it for everyone, but then I remembered, part of what I teach you in this very book is to be endlessly generous. You have to give to get.

If you're ever stressed to death or need a good belly laugh, read my Citizen Kane "The Illuminati Sales Manifesto" to go down that rabbit hole as I satirize every aspect of B2B. It's a jungle out there filled with razor wire and crocodiles, and every one of you wakes up knowing you could be earning 2X, even 5X, but how?

Sales is a game of politics and optics. That's how you actually get ahead.

The world's methods, processes, tactics, and tech stack optimization will not get you to 7 figures. It's one piece. Look at the way this *actually* works. What qualifies me to claim I am a Level 3 Coach is not just that I've advised over 200 tech companies and worked directly with over 1,000 reps.

Coaching Caliber Hierarchy:

- Level I: Doing (most coaching)
  o Tactics & Techniques (average coaching)

- Level II: Thinking (better coaching)
  o Strategy (good coaching)

- Level III: Being (elite coaching)
  o Mindset, Politics & Optics (elite sales leadership)

I advise sellers to treat prospective companies like prospects they're vetting. Execs mistakenly think great sales roles are scarce and sellers are plenty. Flip that paradigm: *you are scarce, and the positions are many.* So much so that many companies are still actively hiring even in the recession. VC funding marches on in endless deployment of dry gunpowder.

Here's the Perfect Role Trifecta from *Codex 17*: You need product-market fit, a great boss, and serious upside. Use compensation benchmarking sites like RepVue, backchannel to sellers that left your target company, and treat getting hired like prospecting. Fill your bench!

Why aren't you cold calling the hiring managers to *show, not tell* why you're the best candidate? Go do it right now. Make it a game and cause a bidding war for your talents. They are vested in recruiting you as you'll rain down revenue with the JMM. Do you know my secret to ensure you always get hired? Confidently state, "My goal is to lead the entire company in cold calling." Game over. "Where do I FedEx you the offer letter, please?"

This information will change your identity and how you think. It's an entirely new operating system for outbound. People will double their income, move from entry-level to Chief Revenue Officer, launch lucrative side hustles, hit President's Club, and earn millions. Marc Benioff put it best, "We overestimate what we can do in 1 year but underestimate what we can do in 10."

Clients I've privately coached, frequently report their best financial year ever and get promoted in under six months more often than not. I've seen the power of coaching endless times. One client, Christian, saw 100% ROI in the first 20 min.

My favorite response is, "Do you guarantee I'll get better?" If you apply what I show you, you will 1000%. Would you rather I give you a fish, a fishing rod, fishing instructions, or give you the keys to a fishing rod factory? Better yet, the blueprints to build the factory!

Break this system to make it your own. Put it to the test. Kick the tires hard and challenge me all day. That's how we improve. Don't listen to vendor surveys or pundits in ivory towers that have never sold. I carried a bag for 20 years and learned from the school of Hard Knocks, PhD - "piled higher and deeper." I traveled the globe with the most badass 7-figure earners who ever lived in technology sales and modeled myself and systems after them. From *COMBO Prospecting* to *Tech-Powered Sales* to the *Codices*.

One thing is for certain, the idea that you can simply "moneyball" your team with specialization or reimagine the primary go-to-market (GTM) functions like Justin Roff-Marsh posits in *The Ma-*

chine, is flawed without factoring in the raw power of OpenAI to disrupt all systems as we know them. Getting rid of commissions and building out enlightened Customer Success Management teams is fatally flawed. Firstly, because "zookeepers that bottle feed the lions, can't hunt them." (hat tip Mike Weinberg). Secondarily, "incentives drive behavior drive revenue" is the principle that built Silicon Valley.

This will blow your mind: Why can't we just replace the entire top funnel with machines, then get the machines to "moneyball" themselves, self-train, and restructure all GTM functions accordingly? Now that's a brave new world and business reality I predict circa 2035 vs. 2025 even at the blistering pace of AI innovation and mergers and acquisitions (M&A).

Where does my knowledge and wisdom come from? Empirical skepticism. 20 years experience in software sales. 20,000+ hours on the phone cold calling. 5MM+ emails sent, $3MM in VC spent A/B testing sequences for 100+ concurrent clients. 200 startups advised, thousands individually coached— real-world lessons from hundreds of millions in revenue driven. *And I'm still learning... every day.* Warning: No sugar coating. My coaching is a blow torch. We will go deeper than you've ever gone before and at last find the root cause holding you back.

GPT Lab: Try out First Principles thinking

Arranging your thoughts with first principles thinking may feel unfamiliar.

Here is a prompt to help you organize your thoughts:

"Consider a common device or process that you use daily, such as a smartphone or your morning routine. Break it down to its most basic, fundamental parts or steps. Now, challenge each of these basic elements. Why are they necessary? Are there any assumptions or conventions that could be questioned or changed? How would you rebuild this device or process from scratch, using only these fundamental parts, but without the constraints of its current form?"

What is coaching?

Here's an insight from a client of mine, Billy Triple, who used the strategies in this book, as well as coaching to get his sales success back on track. Within a few short months, he called me from Vegas, telling me he had already reached "President's Club:

> *"Justin is one of the most genuine people I've crossed paths with in my career. It all started with a cold call from me, which did not turn into a demo but something more substantial: a mentorship. From that day, Justin taught me techniques to set the groundwork for me to succeed. He introduced me to books such as Fanatical and COMBO Prospecting, then would take time out of his day to provide me insights into how to execute these lessons. Looking back, that was the best cold call I ever made. If you are starting a career in sales, I encourage you to contact Justin. Thirty triples a day keeps the PIP away. Preach!"*

Potential is powerful, but it's often meaningless without direction. That's where coaches come in. Success is an inside job - everything you want to achieve is already within you. What a coach does is help you find your inner magic.

Coaches are magicians, mentors, and artists rolled into one.

- We unlock what's dormant within you. Get you unstuck, unblock you.

- We shatter your self-limiting beliefs (and income ceiling).
- We pinpoint unique zones of genius you haven't yet 10X'd.
- We create shortcuts now that only a gifted coach can see.

Deep insight can come in a nanosecond and you are forever changed.

My mentor, Tony J. Hughes, taught me the craft of *strategic selling* in the Enterprise (Fortune 500 companies). As Jim Kreller puts so eloquently, "Deals are different puzzles." I traveled the world with top performers like Garrett MacDonald, Jim Mongillo, and Jim Thoeni. What I learned in this apprenticeship and baptism by fire is not in books, but I'll attempt to capture it here. (Read *Codex 17* for an exact snapshot of a 7-figure mindset. More on this later.)

Coaching is about three things, in my view:

1. Helping clients unlock their potential

Everything you're looking to achieve is already within you: I'm just a faithful sherpa up Mount Everest to help you unlock it - remember 'The Alchemist.'

We all suffer from the same self-limiting beliefs- lies we tell ourselves – especially about money, and general self-deceit, that block our growth personally and professionally. They keep us at a ceiling or plateau. Coaching works to break through these invisible barriers to help us self-inspect to the root cause.

I plateaued for 15 years so you won't have to.

2. Discovering opportunities

We all have areas of unique genius, so a coach can help you pinpoint those and create shortcuts. I bring my 20 years of experience to your problem. 1+1 = 11 when we collaborate, and thus your results quantum leap at warp speed. Behold, the true definition of "synergy."

> *"You already have the ability within yourself to reach your goals." – Dan Kennedy*

3. Providing direction

People enter my bespoke coaching program because they're looking for a system, something they can take and apply immediately.

I'm often asked, "where are your 20 years of experience?" So I keep that link on Crunchbase.com – just search 'Justin Michael' – to quiet down the haters. Yeah, I wouldn't hire that guy, either. What a crappy CV. "He moved around too much," one famous recruiter said to my first clients when I burst on the scene. Then I did my first 100K day, then 200K days became common. Although many won't do this in a year, launching a 10K/mo side hustle kicks off an additional 120K. (Very doable, so what are you waiting for? Let's talk.)

By 2015, after 15 years in sales using these systems, I was generating so much pipeline so fast that I won an Elon Musk 10X Award at a Tier-1 VC-backed Seattle startup with 80MM run rate for 'relentless resourcefulness.' I'd generated six years of pipeline in 6 months and got up in front of 350 people in 8 countries to accept it. I could write my ticket based on my results. My name was completely unknown but I became an anonymous 'cyborg' case study in *COMBO Prospecting* (ComboProspecting.com) by my mentor Tony J. Hughes.

Then Silicon Valley VCs came knocking to build an AI model of my brain while prospecting. With the advent of OpenAI and GPT, it doesn't seem so far-fetched now from a neural network engineering perspective.

Why didn't I stay anywhere long? I mastered top funnel and was in constant demand. I had a multi-offer bidding war every time I switched jobs from then on out, and my base salary reached a ludicrous $250K C-Level baseline, unheard of at the time for an outbound hunter.

As a new business rep, I consistently unlocked more opportunities than everyone except the CRO. This often caused severe enmity until I fed the whole sales org with meetings and trained the SDRs. "Pipeline cures all ills," Kraig Kleeman loves to say. And when you do that, your CRO becomes your best friend and you're the last human standing when the cuts come.

I remained a player-coach all the way up to VP of Sales with a multi-million dollar number on my head running territories out of SF and NYC (I lived in both places) because my CEOs always trusted me with the outbound motion of the entire global business.

A note on fame and infamy: I've been derided, copied, attacked, and Reddit trolled ad nauseam until my LinkedIn profile was flagged and shut off. My techniques have even been declared fraudulent, so I willingly presented my bank statements to one detractor and passed their test with flying colors. I gave away the codex 'cheat code' guides to easily 25,000+ people. Walk your talk.

"The best revenge is massive success." – Frank Sinatra

Countless rivals and 'appointment setting' agencies have grown like gremlins, blatantly stealing my methods without attribution, and scaling 100s of millions in pipeline and revenue off my techniques, never once uttering my name. Some of the most famous people you've ever seen doing outbound training in your LinkedIn feed hijacked my methods without a trace.

I've given away altruistically unlike any other author in business-to-business (B2B) history. All I ask in return is that you use what I provide to your advantage, and maybe share a review or two when these methods make you money.

"Give away the secrets, sell the implementation."
– Alex Hormozi

Emulation is the greatest form of flattery. I was able to excel in the B2B coaching game by 10 years in 3 by going all-in Radiohead free-album status with my intellectual property (IP). It remains an extremely controversial move. But you've gotta ***give to get*** and I guarantee you, the road to seven figures immediately appears if you'll only truly serve others now. Don't wait. Do it today. An abundance mindset is available to all of us in the now.

"You can have everything in life you want, if you will just help other people get what they want." – Zig Ziglar

When I coach, I bring shortcuts to my clients' lives that only I can see. Sometimes the insights I give in seconds help them quantum-leap forward by decades. That's precisely why I coach at the level of insight and being, something unheard of, even alien, in the sales training cottage industry obsessed with surface-level tactics and strategy.

Mindset is important, but it's not enough on its own. We must go deeper to change internal circuitry at a subconscious level.

Like Syd Banks revealed in *The 3 Principles*, there is mind, consciousness and thought and it's up to us to attach meaning to our negative thoughts or drop them. We have 70,000 thoughts per day. When we question what is true á la Byron Katie, we can still our minds, allowing deep insight to emerge from that infinite place of intuition to guide everything we seek. It's the formless coming into form of infinite creativity, ideation and expression all with the deeper motive of true service.

"When you are able to shift your inner awareness to how you can serve others, and when you make this the central focus of your life, you will then be in a position to know true miracles in your progress toward prosperity." – Wayne W. Dyer

Coaching Champions

Being a coach myself has taught me a lot about what it takes to build a champion.

Tech-powered sales enablement and sales management wasn't really talked about in *Tech-Powered Sales* (TPS). When you manage reps you need to get under the hood and look at their sequences. You need to listen to Gong calls with them. Have them pull interesting calls to share with you preemptively before your weekly 1:1.

Any rep can go from good to great if you believe in them. Sales is the transference of belief and effective coaching is unlocking the unlimited potential already inside people. It just takes one caring leader, to lead by example, to believe, and to patiently walk you through what it really takes.

Sales is a sport, it's a verb and action like learning to drive a car, fly a plane, or heli-ski. Good luck learning that in a book. You need to get into the arena and do "reps" just like hitting the heavy bag in the gym - cue your favorite "Rocky" scene.

Back in the day, this was called "windshield time." I'll admit for all the theory I assimilated to break down and build new methods, nothing came close to being in the field with Jim Mongillo, Garrett MacDonald, or Jim Thoeni. You probably don't know these names. They don't have shiny sales books or methods they advertise. But have you ever seen someone do 10MM in 2 years on an ACV of 20K? Legendary.

Find the most successful seller you know, and spend quality time with them. Split your commission on deals and collaborate on closing with them. That's how you'll learn by doing. It will change your life, like it did mine. It's the difference between being a theoretical *challenger* and understanding what this means in reality. Becoming the embodiment of *doing*.

Repetition is the mother of skill.

When we peel back the layers from Doing, to Thinking, to Being within ourselves we find out how the sausage truly gets made on human ability – a core premise of this book. We know in our heart of hearts, what our internal mindset entails (whether we care to ever admit it to anyone else - even coaches, especially superiors).

This is why it's so mission critical to establish trust with top performers we manage so they can open up about their internal circuitry. Do they have impostor syndrome? Where is their self-belief as a barometer for their ability to CLOSE deals? Is there a flood of negative self-talk getting in the way?

For me, the answer was "All of the above."

Many reps are terrified to admit to their manager that they doubt themselves, their deals, or some facet of their ability. While investing in psychotherapy is one way for people to overcome these limitations, there are other options.

Taking "leaps of faith," with the assistance of an experienced senior colleague or manager can be valuable for any growing sales professional. Working with a coach can be a lot like working with a therapist or guide, to overcome limitations.

I've experienced this phenomenon for myself. Back in 2012 when I was still working in Salesforce, I was committed to learning the art of "Enterprise selling." That's a big reason why I sought out the guidance of Tony J. Hughes. It was a crucial driver of my decision to work under the tutorship of people like Jim Mongillo, Jim Thoeni, and Garrett MacDonald.

The power of "others" is something the best salespeople never underestimate. Exposure to new perspectives and concepts is crucial to consistent growth. We need to learn the craft from others who have summited the mountain top, by watching them build out their own strategies.

It's the same as reaching out to an athletics expert when we want to learn how to ski down black diamond hills without breaking our legs. By learning from others, we discover the path we need to take from "beginner" to "champion."

We learn what we should obsess over. For me, it was analyzing the top SDRs and AEs, deconstructing their scripts, calls, and methods to see what was actually yielding results. In studying actual champion reps, you can deconstruct how to become one yourself.

You should never have to fire anyone. Stiffen discipline and they'll usually quit.

The best leaders I had like Jim Thoeni at Salesforce, would ride along with me for big deals. It was amazing doing a renewal with him and learning all the ins and outs of how he negotiated. I really felt supported.

When I reported to Jim Mongillo as GM, I remember my first day he took me to an onsite meeting at Eventbrite. He was deep in the sales cycle with tremendous product knowledge. He also immediately put the stakeholder in the conversation at ease by explaining my presence there: "Justin just joined, he's going to be listening in to learn more about the platform." I took copious notes and it was amazing to learn how stuff actually worked from the viewpoint of the customer.

When you find amazing reps, they will follow you to the ends of the earth and back. I worked for the same few managers and CROs often 2-3 times at multiple companies over many years. So in this case, I became their champion. The biggest reason they kept hiring me is they could trust me to "pick up the phone" which has become symbolic of "doing the hard things every day" and making sales happen.

What motivated me as a champion rep? (Adding this so you do this for your people.)

1. Fight for your sellers' commission
2. Build a Comp Plan that is "pro-sales" vs. CFO as Sales Prevention
3. Get the CFO to stand up in your SKO to explain their enthusiasm to pay the sellers bonuses
4. Travel with your reps in coach
5. Hold 1:1 strategy sessions every week to help advance your sellers' pipelines
6. Champion the seller's goals to the CEO and when they do something awesome, get it in front of the powers that be, management and even the board
7. Provide opportunities for advancement (for Openers, not just Closers)
8. Fight to improve each seller's patch and horse-trade accounts fairly

9. Invest in your seller's tech stacks and training/onboarding - my best managers brought in Challenger, Miller-Heiman, SPIN, TAS and Sandler

10. Give the seller the reins to close the deals vs. "super-closing" so they can gain autonomy, authority, and the power/credibility to marshall deal closes forward

11. Act as a buffer zone in a complex negotiation. If your manager is always stepping in, they can only go to the CRO and then to the CEO. You need a layer of buffer so if the prospect puts pressure on you, you can "check with your manager" within a negotiation. (This doesn't mean giving a guaranteed discount, FYI.)

I'll never forget sitting in board rooms as a Director and RVP scoring deals with TAS - target account selling. I remember when I managed reps, coaching them on a whiteboard to look at who's who in the zoo: frenemy, champion, coach, blocker. Help your people quarterback deals. Strategy is the missing ingredient in effective sales management. Get them to bring you calls that stump them to listen to together.

PART IV: JMM STRATEGY & TACTICS

Sales is the transference of belief. If you have conviction, others will follow suit.

This book details the *modern science of outbound prospecting*. It comprises a series of heuristics (or mental shortcuts) arranged in pillars. To master it, just keep attacking the pillars, and don't forget these foundation elements to boost your success: *COMBO Prospecting* (*I'm the 'cyborg' case study*), *Tech-Powered Sales*, the *Codices*.

Let's address the elephant in the room: You may be uncomfortable implementing this system at first.

Selling is like art; we get used to a specific style. Writing super-short emails, sending imagery in sequences, and using the other strategies discussed here may initially feel unusual. But stay strong, young maverick.

The JMM aims to create "self-actualized" reps that become mini mad scientists, A/B testing everything and making time-tested strategies their own. With this method, it's not just your sales that benefit, but your morale and your team's spirit. Finally, you'll start to feel fulfilled in a job where you once felt like a canary in a coal mine.

You turn outbound from a struggle into a craft and an art form. You start investing in others, learning from them, and enjoying that exchange of ideas. Prospecting becomes learning and growing vs. hustling, grinding, and slogging.

Setting meetings by any channel is about "closing the knowledge gap." Present yourself as a source of guidance and knowledge, not just another salesperson, and you're already on the way to connecting more deeply with your audience.

> *"Look, no hard sell here; let's find some time so I can share our roadmap with you and educate you on the product vision."*

It's a soft sell. It's also an opportunity to prove yourself in that initial meeting. Make that first conversation so good it's worth $200 in 2020's money.

People have always told me my writing, speaking, books, and concepts are too complex, but clients I coach glow. They tell me: "the JMM is so simple and powerful." The lesson I take from this is to believe in your prospect's intelligence. Don't convince yourself you have to "dumb everything down."

Treat people like the geniuses they believe they are.

Decision-makers and real "CEOs of the problem" will flock to you. After all, they're looking for real answers, real value, and genuine insights.

Some apocryphal statistics show that the average CEO reads 60 books yearly, and the average American reads 1. The obvious quest for knowledge among leaders translates to the digital world too. For instance, we know that long-form content online (more than 2,000 words) makes an impact at the executive level.

Catering to the intelligence of your niche sector will serve you far better than putting out "RevOps for Dummies." Be THE voice of your industry that P&L holders must follow.

I'll simplify my thoughts on prospecting, GTM, personal branding, and marketing later. But let's start with this message: You must move from push to pull, chasing to attraction marketing. To quote Jack Canfield's *Butterfly Theory* in *Codex 1*:

> *"The whole industry is obsessed with making bigger, better, faster nets to catch butterflies. Why not, instead, create a garden that attracts them."*

You have two hands to master outbound in any sphere: client creation (prospecting) and fulfillment (delivering value).

You can never stop *prospecting by conversation* for the rest of your life. All conversations lead to deal flow. "Every sale happens inside a conversation," per Rich Litvin. Most entrepreneurs focus 80% of their time on fulfillment or skill-building around their expertise.

When you launch a side hustle or step into a new role, *spend 80% of your time prospecting*. This activity is vital to your ultimate success or failure.

> *"You can get anyone to say yes if you're willing to hear 1,000 No's."* - Byron Katie

Stop tracking metrics like 'meetings held' and sales qualified opportunities (SQOs). Just focus on moving two things North: 1) the amount of no's and 2) the number of "completes" you achieve weekly. More "completes" = more revenue; it's directly correlated. By "a complete" I mean: actually speaking with a prospect.

One more thing: ABI - always be invoicing!

Once my invoicing hit over 200 per year, the floodgates opened. There's no such thing as a "No," only a "Not yet," as Steve Chandler says.

Need a good response to "not in the foreseeable future?"

1) Exhibit high empathy - don't just ignore your prospect. Show them you hear their concerns, understand their pain points, and respect their time.

2) Leave the door open - Make sure your prospect always has an opportunity to change their mind. Remember, most no's are really just "not yet."

Mobile Was My Primary Driver

In a way, I've always been a "friend to the machines." My career path has pushed me to constantly embrace technology, in all of its evolving forms.

Much of my sales experience was forged in the fires of a mobile revolution. Now, we're living in a world where mobile devices dominate our lives. Every day, 80% of our communication happens through these pocket-sized wonders more powerful than a tower computer 20 years ago.

The way we communicate has naturally evolved, with technology paving the way to a new future. Yet, countless salespeople are still living in the past, blasting out extra-formal, expository essay emails, and bulleted lists with reckless abandon.

The human brain struggles to process, remember, and connect with text, yet it's 99% of how we prospect. *Why?*

The problem comes down to an issue with how salespeople are taught and molded by the "experts" that came before them.

We're encouraged to study classic guidelines on how to copywrite. Yet, we all know from our experience interfacing with decision makers who hold P&L (aka our bosses) that formal copywriting isn't really a communication tool.

People don't connect on Slack, LinkedIn, or over SMS with long-winded essays. We chat. We're informal, natural, human.

I remember writing a 3-page email to my CEO as an RVP, Americas, in a Manhattan WeWork. He responded, "If you ever make these over three bullet points again, I won't read it." Another time early in my career, I wrote a big, bold email to my CEO, who responded simply: "rad" in lower case.

Visual, human, and mobile-ready design must be the cornerstone of any outbound system for it to work.

If we are to sell the way in which our customers buy, we must prospect how our customers consume digital and voice communications.

When it's late at night, and you're reading a book; the words get fuzzy as you get sleepy. But if you go to grab an In-N-Out burger, it's mysteriously easy to concentrate on the road and look up at the moon and stars with perfect focus. We painstakingly teach ourselves to read and struggle for years at a young age to get these pesky pictograph symbols down.

The brain can only turn those symbols into images in the visual cortex anyway. We don't want to trigger the lizard brain of our prospects causing 'fight or flight.' It kills trust. Understanding the Limbic Brain, where emotion lives, can help us craft communication hooks that always convert higher than flat, logical messaging.

Rather than base my methodology from others' work, I broke mine down to 'first principles' or the fundamental 'hunting' elements. I almost called it "Venn Selling." It aligns with behavioral psychology, neuroscience, relationship dynamics, persuasion, Game Theory, Social Engineering, and neuro-linguistic programming (NLP). Don't read "sales books" to follow in my footsteps. Spend your time reading deeply on those topics.

The JMM works because it leverages how the prospect's brain optimally seeks to receive communication.

If you think about it, there isn't a single "top of funnel" methodology that fits into the brave new world of LinkedIn's *Sales Navigator,* ZoomInfo, and Outreach as the core tech stack. That's what *Tech-Powered Sales,* my bestseller on HarperCollins co-written by Tony J. Hughes, is all about. (Happy to provide a free email sequence tear-down.)

Look far and wide. You'll find only a sea of templates, one-pagers, tips and hacks. When we get into full-cycle sales subjects like qualification & discovery, negotiation, and closing, traditional methodologies are legion - mostly derived from the 1990s and trace back as far as the 1950s. Todd Caponi would even argue: turn of the 20th century. Most of the best-ever, full-cycle methods provide little to nil novel insight as to what to do with social media or your worn out email tactics and phone openers from yesteryear.

Not only is there nothing new under the sun, if there is a popular phone-based outreach strategy, it's usually just a sentence or two thrown on top of a classic 'opener' as an afterthought for good measure. "This is a cold call, you wanna roll the dice?" Why is that? They all assume you've already "opened" (or secured) a new business opportunity so there's an obsessive focus on strategic progression of deals down the funnel toward negotiation and closing.

These scripts and templates overlook the real problem we all have: getting the meeting/opportunity in the first place!

But opening is the new closing and a friend request accepted is the new opening.

The top funnel is so damn noisy, it's literally becoming impossible to even get the slightest reaction. That's why I'm so big on dialing on "signals" or pre-KPIs like profile views, email opens over 3X (automatically create a task to follow-up in sequencers), and social post interactions (likes, shares, comments).

We all need to find ways to stand out among the noise.

If everyone is using the same email template you are, you will not stand out. That means you have to go beyond the trends. The 2011 Kreuzberger "appropriate person" subject line went so viral, my CEO was getting 5+ per day. If there are 3 or maybe even 9 extrapolated ways to open a cold call, and you're using them all religiously, the prospect expects it.

Your competitors are training them not to respond to you – think about it! As *COMBO Prospecting* so aptly put it, acting naturally (like everyone else) in sales, like boxing, will get you knocked out in the first round.

It's so common to start conversations with: "Hey Justin, how's it going?" or, "Hey Justin, How've you been?"

Sure, the second one is proven to work well but makes me cringe because it's a form of subterfuge. It tries to manipulate people into talking. That's the one style I won't succumb to in this book. Nothing I recommend is grey-hat.

Prospects are smarter than you think. That's why playing up to their intelligence is a lethal pattern interruption. That first *natural* opener is so expected, the usual response is, "Are you trying to sell me something?" And decision makers in SaaS (software as a service) tech ventures have been so buffeted by trite methodologies, some jokingly reply when interrogated, "Are you BANTing me?" to reflect B.A.N.T. – budget, authority, need, and timeline –

a classic 50's era sales qualification methodology popularized in the 90's tech bubble that is remarkably still as ubiquitous as a Swiftie (fan of Taylor Swift).

The ultimate pattern interrupt is always doing something the prospect doesn't expect.

Templates and scripts don't work. Heuristics (mental shortcuts) do. Formulas and frameworks are key.

80% of email gets read on a mobile device, which will only increase, yet 99% of messaging looks like it was built for a 90's-era word processor. Mario Krivokapic writes, "We are still writing emails as if we live in the 1800s, writing IRL (in real life) mail (aka 'letters') to a loved one or a friend. If you think about it:

* * *

Dear [name],

Body

With best regards,

This is how letters were written in the 'before times.'"

The brain processes visual information 60,000 times faster than written and 90% of communication is visual, yet everyone still sends a barrage of little symbols that look like marching ants on little screens to senior executives wondering why the response is so underwhelming.

Not to mention the impossibility of deliverability getting in the way. (The dismal average sequence conversion rate is .5 — half a human?) Suppose you call 100 phone numbers in Enterprise and set 3 meetings. What about the other 97 prospects?

If opening is the new closing, then a 1st-degree connection is the new opening. If the only means to interact is a real-time (RT) direct chat flow, then 4-5 back and forths in a DM is equivalent to a cold call "live connect." Wouldn't you agree?

I've hacked LinkedIn for you: advanced social selling.

I've hacked real-time DM chat frameworks for you. (read The 4th Frame section)

* * *

I'm the first to ever codify this slow dance in B2B. I've seen it called "chat flows" with fitness trainers and life coaches deploying virtual assistants (VAs) on Facebook chat and Instagram DMs but it's never been retrofitted and calibrated for B2B spheres like LinkedIn, Slack and Twitter. I've A/B tested it 'til I was blue in the face and finally found it so you don't have to.

Yes, you will chat with people one by one. And yes, you will like it. ;-)

GPT Lab: Use GPT to test your ability to build pattern interrupts

GPT will help you practice generating these interrupt statements.

Here is a prompt to get you started:

"Imagine you are a person who creates pattern interrupts on starting conversations. What are a few examples of this style of conversation, and why should I use it? Please suggest interrupt styles that are kind and not hurtful."

Targeting on Steroids

"I wholeheartedly recommend working with Justin. During his one-month certification program, we honed my skills in building an outbound pipeline using the Justin Michael Method and basic principles like the 80/20 rule. Justin's teachings are not only relevant to today's market, but they are also based on his extensive experience as a top-performing sales professional.

Not only did I develop a stronger pipeline, but Justin also helped me shift my mindset, particularly in regards to cold calling and engaging with C-level prospects. Thanks to Justin's training, I was able to reach President's Club status with 125%+ attainment in 2022, and I attribute a lot of my success to working with him." – Paul Vorsmann, Account Executive, HubSpot

> *"Give me six hours to chop down a tree and I will spend the first four sharpening the ax."*
>
> *– Abraham Lincoln*

Targeting is everything. If outbound sales is like archery, the bow is sequencing and the arrow is messaging. So many talking heads hyper-focus on messaging bringing 10X. But it won't do anything if your targeting is bad. Measure twice, cut once. When campaigns don't work, do boolean list pulls and groom your data until it's

98% clean. Focus on contacts who have a high probability to be in a buying window.

"The list is the strategy." – Joey Gilkey

So obsess over gaining clean data that is "human-verified."

Hemingway's *Old Man and the Sea* could be the best prospecting book of all time. Why? "Be the ball," as notorious pro golfer Ty Webb would say in *Caddyshack*. Be the fish. Understand a day in the life of who you are targeting. Your ability to empathize and put yourself directly into your prospect's shoes to walk a mile is the biggest determinant of outbound success and obtaining "message market fit." It allows you to A/B test every possible channel and tactic until you find streaks and they "bite."

While you'd expect a vast exercise on buying personas (we put that into *Tech-Powered Sales*), I've come to think of targeting as finding a title cloud or title array. The best way to determine your ICP when you enter a company is to look in the rearview mirror. Perform a Craig Elias "won-sales analysis." This reveals patterns like, "Wow, looks like the CRO, CISO, Head of IT, and Controller are the most frequent titles we see over and over in these deals."

The second most obvious place to find immediate clients is your top 5 competitors' case studies, testimonials, or logo wall. Or, run on "look-alike" lists you build off your best customers by vertical. The human brain's ability to *rapidly* do pattern recognition and glean insight will far exceed AI for a long while:

Here's how you assess where you WON:

- *Look at your case studies, highest revenue customers, most upsold, longest retained, and happiest customers*

- Go run through the deadwood of "closed-lost opportunities."
- Run a "where are they now?" manually on every single contact/prospect associated with those old deals in your CRM. Go find them on LinkedIn *now*.
- Take the last 50 contracts signed (closed-won) and find the stakeholders. Look 'em up: track job changes. Better bond with your CFO to get permission to do this!
- Analyze their job title, persona, and drivers of the sale (in their own words.) Seek out patterns and triggers.
- Leverage this intel in your outbound going forward.
- Mine your install base to ask for referrals and leverage the networks of your best customers for pathways into look-a-like accounts (all easily done in Sales Navigator via "Connections of <Name>")

I always do this in the first 90 days of a new prospecting endeavor. Right now, it's very possible to improve targeting based on technology, intent, and other triggers.

Take the time to look at the new accounts in your data providers & Sales Nav, not just your CRM. Sometimes your expectations don't match reality, but looking in depth can unearth hidden patterns behind the best accounts.

Systems exist to find out which technographics your prospects use, figure out which accounts (even contacts) are searching for your solution, and find ways to monitor job changes, funding etc. Navigator is hugely helpful for this, as are BuiltWith and Similarweb. Technographic drops build insane credibility. "Hey, Noticed you're using Snowflake in your tech stack. Our solution integrates..."

With the advent of AI, privacy controls and regulation will get stronger, but the tools will find ways to get around this. It's a constant game of whack-a-mole.

Think about how you can use platforms to understand who's already in the buying window, and who's using tech stacks that integrate well with yours. You can even run "nearbound" campaigns in CrossBeam or Reveal to open up a mutual opportunity list by syncing the data in your overlapping CRMs to co-sell as you go-to-market. Speak to this in your messaging. Understand which trigger events will always be most powerful.

The most crucial trigger event is a "job change." I learned this initially from Craig Elias of "Shift! Selling," written over a decade ago. He documented that CXOs new to the role, deploy 1 million in capital to shake up their tech stacks. Another massive determinant of churn is the relationship to the account, like if the incumbent account manager leaves – so watch for that.

"Buyers buy."

I came up with this Yogi Berraism. Across 13 startup companies where I led top line revenue efforts, I'd often open a deal at one company with a prospect and close it 2, even 3 years later, while selling similar technology at another. Buyers buy because 3% of the market is in the buying window per the Chet Holmes Pyramid, and 40% will entertain switching. Your competitors' customers understand their buying process vs. chipping away at someone who's never bought before, something I call "the religious sale."

Once in North Idaho, my customer said, "Justin, wherever you go, I buy from you." The Blountism, 'people buy you,' rang so true then. Gartner research has always borne out that 'the experience with the seller' is the only true differentiator as all markets are now commoditized. Software has indeed "eaten the world," (Marc Andreessen) and all solutions are perceived in parity.

Of course, there are various triggers like funding rounds, hiring, technology innovation, M&A, and geographic expansion. Funding triggers have gotten so played out that whenever someone lands financing, they get bombarded with emails applauding them like roaches when the lights go out. Congratulating people on promotions or job changes doesn't work anymore. Who wants a stranger back-slapping them? E.g. "Congrats on becoming a CMO, that's amazing," a rep writes. When in reality: CEO to CMO, "You have 3 quarters max to turn this business around, or you're fired."

Tony J. Hughes talks about the 3 states of business: growing, flat or decay. Flat and decay are the same. Only sell to companies in affluence: this means monitoring headcount growth (sometimes "hiring" is illusory and just for optics) so find out if they're profitable. In publicly traded companies, this is easy to deduce but for the private sector, you'll have to put on your detective hat and do some digging.

One of the best places to find hidden triggers is in "recent activity." Profiles that look dead on LinkedIn are often just executive lurkers with explosive action on "recent activity:" liking and commenting. You can find clues there to personalize your messaging or understand buying triggers, pain points, etc.

That said, the best time to strike is still in that window just after the job change because an incoming executive will have the latitude and budget authority to switch up significant pieces of their tech stack.

This is when Pardot gets ripped out for Marketo or vice versa. This is where the CRM battles and email automation wars are won and lost. This is where you do the 6 figure, 2-year deal to rip out their existing sequencer, data provider, and conversational intelligence – all at once – with a "reduction of total cost of ownership (TCO)" positioning.

Triggers make my life so much easier as an effective cold caller. "Jane Smith?" "No, it's Chuck Woolery." "Oh, I had been reaching out to Jane about marketing automation, is that you now?" "Yes, what's up?" Boom, you're in.

One of the best triggers is "prospect visited site." With site deanonymization tech you can track specific I.P. ranges or domains that come in. I know one Enterprise Seller who reviews the inbound URLs daily to suss out who's in the buying window. Sometimes that's Accenture or Deloitte level. You can also have your reps sitting in front-site chat bots like Drift or Chat Metrics to interact in real-time when available or set ChatGPT-enabled AI chat bots on this, after hours.

MULTI-THREADING

"If you're not multi-threaded you're deaded."

It's so crucial to multi-thread even the smallest account. You need to establish multiple pathways in. Top-down, middle-out, bottom-up and all at once. This is the "art of confusion." If you go in high at the C-Level only, they may block you from the VPs. If you go in at Director or VP, they may get upset if you go around them to contact their boss.

CEOs are often "CE-No's." Even if you get blocked at the top, keep multithreading middle out, bottom-up to create groundswell and consensus. I can't tell you how many C-Suite executives laugh once I'm face to face in their board room or on a Zoom after having already rejected me and I cleverly orchestrated a campaign to get back on their radar.

I've discovered breakthroughs in frequencies depending on hierarchy while threading, largely inspired by Steven W. Martin at USC Marshall School of Business. Utilizing COMBO 'triples,' sequencing, and blended omnichannel approaches is always the best practice.

Effective outbound works as a series of plays combining channels in myriad ways. Document and test everything. Then like a sports head coach, build and execute a scalable, repeatable playbook to create predictable revenue.

Personally, I never work more than 200 accounts at a time. The 80/20 rule means I'm often focusing mostly on 40 key accounts, or 20%. I'd run manual or semi-auto strategies on those VIP "front burner" accounts. Then, with the back burner, or 160 *other* accounts, I'd run full-blown sequence automation. Understanding how to use Manual (COMBOs) and Autonomous (*Tech-Powered Sales*) simultaneously will give you the most leverage, traction and reach.

When I used to sell Sales Navigator from the Empire State Building, I'd build groundswell demoing the product to the front line sellers, then arrange group demos with VPs, but also work the C-Levels, often multi-country (where we sometimes already had MSAs in place to speed the process).

The best story I can refer to here comes from the CMO of Marriott who placed a quote in Wired magazine about their new hotel mobile app. I was using geofencing technology at the time that was so accurate, you could trigger different offers at the pool or the lobby vs. drawing one fence around the whole hotel property.

I sent her a quote in an email on a Friday afternoon at 7pm Eastern as part of a Triple: call, VM, email. She responded immediately based on that contextually "relevant" personalization with a suggestion on leveraging the geofence tech. I was then routed to England. The next day England responded linking me to Dallas and within 2 weeks I was on a plane to Plano, Texas to meet with their customer experience (CX) team. And this was a Fortune 500 using multiple competitors. Multi-threading and working an account top down!

When in doubt, always call in high at the C-Level. I stake my name on it because I built my career on this bold trajectory. Do not waste your time safely talking to people that can only say "no."

We get delegated down to who we sound like, so we must tailor our messaging at the C-Level to "outcomes and risk." Lower down, specific technical use cases and features make more sense to lean on. Try not to get too "in the weeds" when communicating with senior buyers. They'll probably just shuffle you off into an IT blackhole. You can do an entire deal off one use case, something I call "enterprise use case selling." It's not a feature but the flow of features rolled up into a use case or customer story that drives results.

We did a 7-figure deal on this, leveraging the ability for an airline to do immediate interactive surveys with push notifications upon landing vs. waiting 24 hours. This instantaneously increased engagement to over 85% from under 5%. What's that worth to an airline for customer satisfaction (CSAT) and net-promoter score (NPS) improvements? Everything.

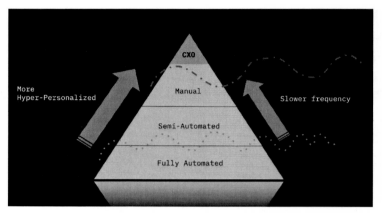

Hyper-personalized flow up to CXO

The personalization pyramid is a simple but mighty concept. The higher up you go on the organizational map, the slower the frequency of messaging and the more "hyper-personalized" you need to make the messages. Would you send the CMO of T-Mobile a 27-touch sequence? Nope. In fact on the first email, I got an auto-responder to "please take me off the list." With many other CXOs, an Executive Assistant (EA), is running interference on all their inboxes, including social.

The debate rages on: personalization vs. relevancy. Personalization is the wrong North Star because it risks lowering your status. It's created via curly brackets in systems like Salesloft and Outreach that fill in parameters at scale creating sentences like this: "Hey Bill, I see your headcount grew by 50." Problem is, every recipient knows it's automated by now.

Hyper-personalization is my vote which has been called "customization" by Jeremey Donovan at Insight Partners (formerly SVP, Sales Strategy at Salesloft). A great example is stating, "When you shared <quote> at minute 6 and 22 seconds in your recent podcast on TechCrunch, it really resonated with <this aspect> of what our product is solving."

Testing on 6MM anonymized emails at Salesloft, Donovan found that 20% personalization at the front of the sequence is all that's needed. "Needy is creepy" per Steve Chandler. This matches Aaron Ross's recommendation on using up to 20% personalized messages in cadences. CEOs often report, "If you check out my Instagram, it weirds me out." Stay focused on "work relevance" down to the industry and title (persona) not necessarily the individual within your ICP. RELEVANCE is the economic graph (think LinkedIn) vs. PERSONALIZATION resembling the social graph (think Meta-Facebook).

Personalization by definition cannot scale. It's an oxymoron. How could anything that scales be personal? Personalization looks needy, and need is creepy.

Where GPT technologies need to evolve is in the ability to use NLP (natural language processing), to parse out minute 6 and 22 seconds of a podcast for hyper-personalization – and reference that insight in the front of a tailored prospecting email. Imagine utilizing an AI to listen to your prospect's podcasts at scale while pulling out the most potent nuggets for personalized sequence injection. Power!

I've always said, "personalize on something a machine wouldn't find" but with the advent of ChatGPT, machines are becoming serious sleuths. That's why your ability to synthesize, which is really an artistic process, becomes so important. In an AI-enabled prospecting world, remember:

You're no longer differentiating your messaging against competitor reps. You're differentiating your messaging against your competitor's AIs.

Many sellers come up dry on an entire account. It's like taking blood from a stone; no one is responding. Here's an advanced technique called "flanking" that can help. When you're doing targeting for a campaign, it's about pulling in titles that are lateral or oblique to your direct ICP.

In the good ol' switchboard days, we'd call the sales team to gain intel because they'd always pick up. We'd then use those insights to call the marketing team and higher ups to talk "mobile strategy." This still works! But flanking can also mean using the "People Also Viewed" section on any standard LinkedIn profile to the lower right; it's often blocked because it's so powerful.

The Napoleonic strategy of asymmetric warfare is the original guerrilla approach. When you can't crack an account directly, start to pull lateral titles to the ICP, even HR and especially the sales team. Napoleon figured out how to leverage the element of surprise and come in on angles in configurations and at times the enemy would never suspect. Get your hands on some Robert Greene books like *33 Strategies of War* to apply these timeless principles to matrixed account penetration.

Example: Two office supply giants merged and I was suddenly selling a crowdsourcing data platform. I needed to get to the Chief Digital Officer (CDO) and he was impossible to reach — I must have made 50 calls, emails, and LinkedIn messages to no avail.

I ended up looking at "People Also Viewed" and finding the VP of Financial Planning & Analysis. "Vern" picked right up, understood my business case from an ROI perspective, and gave me the cell phone number of the CDO. Within 2 weeks we were in Boca Raton doing a 6-figure deal.

The beauty of that meeting is we brought screenshots of aspects of his e-commerce site that were broken as our presentation. He shot dagger looks at his head of E-Comm in the boardroom. We got the business and I'm not sure the leader got fired, but he was moved to another division. None of this would have been possible without insight into the "people also viewed" hidden algorithm. For some reason I've never seen explained, the people your prospect is closest to (communicates with the most) are displayed there even if they're at another company. It's like a virtual water cooler revealer. Trust it, try it.

Have a bad patch or a super limited strategic patch?

For a bad patch, you'd work every possible account in the list. I once ended up selling Sales Nav to a giant French water conglomerate, putting on a hard hat in a factory in Philly and convincing them municipal government representatives were on social. These sales execs didn't even use LinkedIn.

But as soon as they saw the opportunity to directly connect to 10-20 year government water contracts, they were supremely interested. I would never have ranked that account as one to travel to but I learned quickly, "there are no bad patches; just inconsistent approaches." Think of your patch like a beach, first turn over every rock then use the "currency of interactivity" as a reason to stack rank your Account-Based Sales Development (ABSD) tracker (shared Google sheet) and go deeper in the prioritized accounts that raised their hand.

Maybe you're saying, "But I only have 15 key accounts and my only job is to penetrate them and create a paid proof to concept (POC)."

This happens more frequently than you think in Enterprise. This happens with Strategic Account Executives or Major Account Sellers. In these situations, take the time to map out the power base of the account in Lucid or some other flowchart software: friends, enemies, frenemies, blockers. It's like running a political campaign. You need to speak to two dozen people in this account and find the people that will drive consensus.

Send books, gift cards to Amazon, wine, coffee, whatever you have to do to evoke thoughtfulness and Cialdini reciprocity. Remember, graft/bribery laws limit gifts typically to under $25. Being extremely hyper-personalized and strategic, sending VITO ("very important top officer") style FedEx letters with a business case, social proof, and a time you'll call works. CXOs always open FedEx and at this writing it's worth the $35. Hat tip Tony Parinello.

GPT Lab: Summarizing content for reuse

Context is everything when reaching out to a buyer.

When you find an article that piques your interest, cut and paste the first 250 words into GPT and ask it to summarize and provide a few top points in just a few words. Then, ask it to simplify the language and make it less formal.

You'll get a great snippet to add to an email or call.

COLD CALLING 3.0 TO INFINITY

"Two of my BDRs doubled their outbound meetings 30 days after implementing the Justin Michael Method. Justin's methods are unique. In a niche, competitive market, standing out and being different is important. His methods cut through the noise.

His calling method is something I've never experienced before. Our reps are getting to meetings a lot faster. When not booking meetings, they get 10X the amount of information and 2X the number of referrals.

This isn't a basic framework for prospecting. This is advanced. If your reps get decent results using a basic prospecting system, this will boost it. Also, keep an open mind; a lot of his stuff comes across a bit out there, but it works." – Daniel Herbert, Director of Sales, Q4

Why is prospecting so damn hard for so many? Lack of pipeline is a universal pain, so I've dedicated my career to fixing it. It's another paradox - the people most responsible for generating pipeline results have the most anxiety, fear, call reluctance, and stage fright. It's a silent epidemic that inflicts 10MM tech sellers, 400MM small business owners, and probably 50MM go-to-market executives across all functions.

Let's do the math for a second. My mantra repeated in this book flips the script: *you are scarce and your prospects are legion.*

It's a good mentality to adopt in a world of sellers with impoverished thinking. It replaces the thought: "My patch is dried up; there's no one left to engage."

You must embrace this "abundance and prosperity mentality" as you prospect. Every seller needs to earn new clients *consistently,* but they don't always prospect effectively and consistently. We all have moments when we lack confidence, self-esteem, and a scalable, repeatable, predictable system.

Mastering this game is like mastering fitness: "The heaviest weight you'll ever lift is the door to the gym." Being physically out of shape is a lethal combination of a) lack of physical activity and b) habitual eating of the wrong things. Similarly, an anemic pipeline consists of a) lack of prospecting and b) when we do it, we're going about it with all the wrong behaviors.

Like weight loss, the barriers to success lie within our mindset, self-esteem, and self-limiting beliefs. We are, in essence, holding ourselves back. But what if we could get out of our own way and learn to fly again?

Fears related to money and power, combined with a lack of confidence, often permeate our psyche. Sometimes we're unaware of these inner barriers, or it comes from some trauma in our childhood that is still unresolved.

It's not laziness or lack of discipline. Those are symptoms of a larger issue. Sellers fear POWER; they shy away from calling CEOs.

They go beta, aim low, and produce even less. Why? Bottom line: they are afraid. They secretly fear prospecting. Humans can only act out of fear or love – it's like the Force in Star Wars – so it's up to you to choose. We're going to solve all that and more in this book. I was once just like you. I know how debilitating fear can be, but I also know how important it is to learn to overcome it.

Alongside fear, the second biggest reason for failure is a lack of business acumen. However, one of my first mentors, who sold his venture to Larry Ellison, used to assure me when I was 27, struggling to get Executive Directors on the phone all day, "How you speak adds ten years to your age."

When I developed my signature cold calling method in 2007, I closed 37 deals in a row on the first call.

But closing deals in the first call isn't simple.

We live in the new era of 'death by committee' or 'every decision by consensus,' so it will be near-impossible to close on a first call.

Route-Ruin-Multiply (RRM) works well because the prospect is spotlighted and opens up often in a couple of minutes, sometimes even for 10 to 20.

With this strategy your prospect comes to your meeting far more open and amenable, far more likely to jump at your offer and get in on the ground floor with you and your business. Your proposal shoots up in their estimation, making them much more excited to achieve the dreams you are laying out before them.

The immediate breakthrough here is the polarity shift.

Before the advent of the JMM Strategy, cold callers interrupted prospects, fire-hosed them with schpiel, and drowned them with "reasons for the call." This lowered their status in the eyes of the prospect.

They were shooting themselves in the foot from the word 'go.'

This violation of basic phone etiquette invariably produces prospect resistance and hang-ups. Why? Listening controls calls, nothing else.

We only need two ideas to control a call opener or any human interaction for that matter:

- Listening - The prospect must talk more than we do; let them lead the conversation with your prompting.
- Questioning - Get your prospect involved in your conversation upfront and make your pitch later.

But how do you do this? How do you effectively hand over your sales call to your prospect?

RRM: Route-Ruin-Multiply or RRR: Route-Ruin-Rip

1. State their full name (Dale Carnegie's "most beautiful sound in the human language")
2. Ask an open question to trigger their power and get them talking

   a. "Who's in charge of your [specialty] strategy?" [ROUTE]

      I. I am

         - Great, how do you currently do this?
      ii. They mention they do it internally or with a competitor
         - Agree and validate

            a. "You're ahead of the game; how's that working out for ya?"
            b. "They're great; how's that working out for ya?"

3. Be genuinely curious about their situation to:
    a. Find THE problem [RUIN]
    b. Create desire
    c. It disarms them by asking what they *like* about the incumbent (status quo), and they admit to issues
    d. If you find pain, peel it - don't immediately bandage it. Poke the wound and twist the knife. "I like Acme, but their customer service is bad." "Oh really, bad in what way? What's the impact?" [study SPIN]
    e. TIME traveling: If they say, "We use Acme; we're good," you go back in time with, "When did you install Acme?" "What other solutions did you evaluate?" This creates cognitive dissonance between the pain they used to have vis-a-vis now (maybe they didn't fully solve it). That delta emotionally triggers them – reminds them of lingering pain – and you can extoll the value of your solution to solve it more fully and close the gap *now*.

4. Once desire is strong, the polarity shift occurs
    a. Pitch the MULTIPLIER
    b. Book the meeting
    c. "Why not plug us in alongside your current solution to *multiply the effectiveness* of your fraud reduction?"

5. RRR: Route-Ruin-Rip
    a. In the pitching phase, you just straight-up pitch with a strong, unique value proposition that is differentiated, but it works because they're interested in hearing it. Products like IT, phone systems, CRMs, or hardware often require a "rip-and-replace" strategy, because they don't augment an existing stack.

The "polarity shift" is what we seek. We must first implant the desire for your product or service into the prospect's brain. It has to be their idea to go into business with you. By being curious enough towards them, they become interested in you. Only by being infinitely *interested* do we become *interesting*. This is also called *Vampire Rule*, only *they* can invite you over the threshold to inevitably pitch.

Opportunities will always swing towards sellers when they genuinely search for ways to help and support their customers.

We will forever push on a rope if we pitch from the front of calls, suffocating our prospects. These simple realizations supersede Route-Ruin-Multiply (RRM) because by following them axiomatically, the phrasing doesn't matter. Any series of words will work as long as you:

- Lead with their full name
- Begin with an open question
- Remain genuinely curious (and fully present) throughout the conversation
- Flip polarity (it becomes their idea)
- Delay the instant gratification of immediate pitching.

Through these methods, even the slightest spark or ember of pain, irritation, or latent pain is probed and excavated for root causes that will aid you in building a stronger relationship with each lead.

After all, it's the relationship that really matters.

Stop obsessing over selling your product. Instead, you should stay focused on the ROUTE you need to follow: "Who should I talk with?" > "What do they need?" > "How can I deliver value?"

Unfortunately, decades of modern selling techniques have helped prospects to develop new instincts when it comes to cold calling. Human beings now have a modernized version of the lizard brain, finely tuned after 200 million years of evolution to detect bullshit.

Selling has changed, you say? Email is dead? Phone is dead? It's just not true. If our brains are the same, then the ways they're manipulated can't have changed much.

This version of our brain evolved over the last 2 million years. It's identical to the brain we had 100 years ago and will remain intact 100 years from now if we don't annihilate ourselves via AI or nukes.

The brain has developed an interesting defense mechanism against salespeople. It tells people to lie to salespeople to eliminate them. Over time, this has developed into another frustrating practice: prospects agree to a meeting, without any intent of showing up, or listening to what you have to say.

It's a bad ecosystem, and the problem stems from us, as sellers, taking the wrong approach, and focusing too heavily on the sale.

I'm vehemently against using PBOs (permission-based openers) for these reasons. "Can I get X seconds of your time?"

The theory is like the "negative labeling" Voss construct: "If I pattern-interrupt by getting a prospect to say 'no,' they will convert." Some examples of this particular technique include:

- Opening phone calls with "Did I catch you at a bad time?"
  o The prospect replies, "No," and you can continue.
- When writing an email, begin with "Would you be opposed to meeting at 1pm on Thursday?"

o The prospect replies, "No," and you can book an appointment.

But as with many of the classic techniques, prospects are growing immune to this strategy. They've been exposed to the same old sales "tricks" for too long.

If you want to capture that deal, you need to think outside of the box with how you open the sale. The opening - the first impression you make on your prospect - defines your ability to build a real relationship.

Beginnings are important.

Studies show that while it only takes between 33-100 milliseconds for someone to form a first impression about another human being, it's almost impossible for us to change the impression we make.

When you start your relationship with a prospect from a subservient position, suggesting you're not worthy of their time, or that you don't have amazing value to offer, they'll continue to believe that about you going forward.

The aim is to get customers to trust you and, more importantly, act on your suggestions and advice. This means you should constantly commit to presenting yourself as an authority - a source of genuine knowledge and insight.

You are not a server cautiously approaching a table to ask, "Still or sparkling?" You are an equal and trusted advisor.

Never forget this. It affects tonality and body language. Most experts in behavioral psychology agree that 70-90% of communication is nonverbal, and 10% is what you say.

So, how exactly do you exude the right image and make the best first impression? Most salespeople will tell you it's all about confidence. In sales, just like relationships, confidence can be highly seductive.

However, it's also something many prospects have come to expect. If you do exactly what your customer expects of you, you're less likely to capture their attention.

So how do you exude confidence the right way?

With the JMM, you'll keep your tone and attitude neutral. Imagine you're working in Air Traffic Control or the Departmet of Motor Vehicles (DMV).

I started experimenting with this when I did Red Bull cold call competitions in my late 20s. Making 3am Pacific calls to bleary-eyed prospects on the Eastern Seaboard in the dark requires a different tact.

Being calm-voiced was initially about preventing burnout, but I started to notice some interesting results. Whether hungover, sick, or tired, a stoic tone beat out all the salesiness and commission breath from my voice.

While focusing on getting your tone right, think about your listen-to-talk ratio.

When I audit calls, I frequently notice sellers aren't self-metering: they often talk too long or ask ultra-long questions. When you speak, it's a hot potato in your hand.

Keep the focus on your prospect.

Listening reduces the friction between you and them. Agreement or validation increases connection and attention. In essence, it's non-judgmental: you take the walls down and disarm prospects by acting differently toward them than every other seller.

The Principle of Disinterest (Non-Hunger) remains in full effect.

You can't smother or show neediness towards your prospect; that repels the sale.

What's really killing your deals? They sense your *need*. That's what you need to kill in your tone. Reverse your paradigm: Imagine everyone is trying to buy from you and you're just processing orders all day. How blunt would you be? Imagine you weren't even paid commission.

Sample notes from a recent coaching session listening to calls – advice to my client:

- remove salesiness from your tone (no commission breath)
- listen to people really closely and respond in the moment with the appropriate acknowledgments
- listen deeply without an agenda to move to pitching at the precise moment (even wait for 5-10 minutes)
- focus on the quality of your questions (implication and need-payoff questions - 2nd order value in SPIN, "what are the consequences if you don't change?" - "how would this pay off for you financially if you fixed it?")

Aaron Ross calls the first call AWAF: "are we a fit?" I like this positioning because the seller is trying to "qualify out the customer" and that truly puts you in the right mindframe to nail your TONE. vs. "I'm *trying to sell you* this pen."

Tell don't sell.

"To be a trusted advisor you only need 2 things: trust and advice." – Iannarino

It's the same reason I've advocated never to ask for a callback on a voice message. You might be eager to earn your customer's attention, but showing too much eagerness sends the wrong impression. It dilutes your value.

Instead of constantly begging for attention, focus on taking advantage of the attention you already have. If you write an email and a customer opens it, they're already "on the hook." You don't always need to ask for a meeting straight away. Sometimes you can just lay the foundations for a conversation.

Taking this "laid back" approach to sales may seem difficult when you're targeting bigger companies and clients. However, the bigger the target, the more critical a neutral approach will be.

Remember that Fortune 500 companies are like supermodels. When you're going after a whale, you can't sit there fawning over them.

They expect that, and most find it to be a major turn-off.

Hence why I sarcastically call it HomegenousGPT because it hasn't solved for "fawning" and it all sounds alike.

Ten thousand *approved* sales trainers taught us to be confident in a bygone era: to stand up straight, hold our shoulders back, and power pose. They told us to put on a suit and tie at our standing desk, squeeze a stress ball, or brandish a putter like Corporate Bro.

Honestly, it's an outdated concept. Worse - it's a cliché.

If doing your best "Mad Men" impersonation on the phone is so necessary, then how was it possible for me to set world records like "six years of pipeline in 6 months" or win the 10X award for Relentless Resourcefulness from Tune.com, all in a quiet, calm, gentle voice?

The reality is, an obnoxiously confident tone doesn't break barriers anymore. It's frustrating and annoying. The more value you place on your voice with a bold tone, the more attention you take away from the person you should be listening to.

Remember, sales conversations aren't about you. They're about getting your prospect to open up and keeping them hooked.

Your prospect will get to know you, your products and services, and your values naturally as you progress through a truly engaging conversation.

They'll learn whether they can trust you based on the quality of your questions.

If you learn RRM and how to get prospects talking first to shift polarity, the floodgates begin to open on your cold-calling abilities—speed to trust quantum leaps. Just ask Luke Ruffing, who took Rookie of the Year at PandaDoc and then went to "President's Club" for three straight years in a row using ROUTE openers alone.

The conversation becomes less about you "pitching a product" and more about actively showing your prospect what's in it for them (WIIFM).

'Sales' is not something you *do* to someone. You can't bully someone into spending their money - certainly not in this economy.

Effective sales is about learning how to _serve_ your prospect. It's about helping your prospects uncover their true problems when we peel back the onion of symptoms to the actual root cause. This takes deep listening coupled with humility, humanity, and empathy.

So, be curious. Call your prospect by name, and ask them questions that invite them to talk about themselves. Find out if you're talking to the right person by asking: "Who's in charge of your [content optimization] strategy?" or for Europe, "Who handles your [whatever]?" to soften. Insert any specialty you focus on in those brackets.

When they say, "I am," it is the most powerful human language phrase. It's the first two words God said when he created the world in many traditions.

You allow your prospect to take ownership of their identity, the conversation, and decision-making ability.

The second biggest way to interrupt the pattern in a traditional sales call is to begin agreeing with your prospect more often.

If they say they already use a competitive solution, tell them what you know about that solution, admit it has good features, and validate their original decision. It's easy to enter kill mode as a seller and try annihilating our competitors.

But berating your customer for making the "wrong" choice with their first purchase won't convince them you have the better solution. It just makes them question their own abilities, and diminishes their confidence. What's more, it makes your prospect defensive. It immediately encourages them to stand up for themselves, and argue about why their solution is better than whatever you offer.

This sets you up for a combative conversation where you have to work even harder to pitch your solution. Your sales call shouldn't be a debate.

Once you've validated their decision and recognized its value, you can start sowing the seeds of doubt.

Enter the "RUIN" step of the RRM model:

"Oh, that's great. I've heard awesome things about [product] - how is it working out for you?"

RRM follows a process that looks like crossing the Panama Canal. Each lock gets filled with water, and your boat moves to the next. So if you haven't found out "who's in charge," – re-route. Ask it again, "Who heads up your analytics strategy? Does that roll up to you?" Even re-route again, slightly altering the question each time.

Accordingly, in the RUIN step, you must dig to the heart of their problem and experience a polarity shift before you pitch a multiplier.

If your prospect says they're happy with their solution and everything is going well, dig deeper. Ask about specific features. Question which goals they've accomplished and what they've failed to achieve.

Convince them to examine whether they're really happy with the product or just trying to avoid a sales call.

The steps of my frameworks are like a safe crack combination, rotating the knob delicately until the pin clicks.

Despite the modern customer journey and communications being non-linear, you can still bring linearity to the process. In fact, doing so exerts positive control factors and a strong frame (Oren Klaff) that will allow you to lead, maintain equilibrium and keep the upper hand even as the prospect attempts to dominate you.

I always compare traditional cold calling to Kung Fu's fast hands and blocking. Alternatively, the Justin Michael Method is more like Aikido, Judo, or Jiu-Jitsu - leveraging your opponent's energy to your advantage.

Once you've convinced your prospect to start questioning their decision and they are open to exploring other options, you can pitch your "multiplier." In other words, start drawing more attention to the challenges they face. Ask them to evaluate the real impact of having the wrong solution and quantify their losses.

From here, you can use your own solution as a comparison point, showcasing how your offering will eliminate the pain points they've already admitted to facing. *"Why not plug us in alongside your current solution to multiply the effectiveness of your marketing automation?"*

It might sound like a relatively passive or introverted approach to selling, but who really sells better: Introverts or Extroverts? It's the proverbial Matthew Pollard question. The ability to lead and guide trumps all, and you don't need to be an extrovert to guide someone.

A common sales myth is that confident sellers always win. Overconfidence repels the modern consumer. Remember, you're dealing with buyers who already believe they know everything. They don't want to speak to someone who belittles their intelligence.

Taking an introverted approach doesn't have to mean being shy and nervous. Instead, it's about bringing serenity and calm in a chaotic world.

Trusted advisors and effective salespeople take the backseat in the sales conversation. They actively listen and use questions to guide the conversation.

If a rep can't guide, they won't close.

Matthew Dixon & Ted McKenna's, *The JOLT Effect*, is an excellent reminder to remove indecision through leadership vs. "endlessly re-litigating the status quo."

Leadership and guidance are what prospects truly crave as the antidote to their 'indecision.' Sometimes, this means combining introverted and extroverted practices. Knowing when to stand back and when to stand up in a boardroom rather than meekly scribbling notes is essential.

So, how do you know the RRM model has worked?

There are a few signs:

1) The call extends to 10-20 minutes (cut them off at ten and just pitch)
2) Your prospect asks permission to bring their boss to the next meeting
3) Your prospect sets the next call, providing their calendar information for you to work with (can you even imagine?!)

Before moving to voicemails, you can find a complete cold call example of implementing the JMM below.

The cold caller is on the left, and the prospect is on the right for easy navigation.

Step 1: Intro

> *"Is this Nancy Kowalczik? Koh - wal - chik."*
>
> > *"Yes"*
>
> *"Hey, It's Justin Michael from Acme Corp."*

Step 2: Route

> *"Just curious... Who's in charge of your CX strategy?"*
>
> > *"Why, what's this about?"*
>
> *"I have some CX tech but don't want to waste your time... just curious who heads up CX, does that roll up to you?"*

Step 3: Ruin (Peel the Onion)

> > *"Yes"*
>
> *"How do you do that now? Do you handle it internally or work with a 3rd party?"*
>
> > *OPTION 1:*
> >
> > *"Oh, we actually build internally..."*
>
> *"Oh, did you choose to do that or someone there before you? // How long did it take you to build it out?"*
>
> > *OPTION 2:*
> >
> > *"We already have a vendor"*
>
> *"Makes sense - who do you use?"*
>
> > *WON'T DISCLOSE:*
> >
> > *"Can't say"*
>
> *"Oh, interesting... what do you like about them? [Then shut up...]"*
>
> > *THEY NAME THE VENDOR:*

"It's Beta Corp"

"Beta Corp is great; how's that working out for you? [pregnant pause... Wait]"

THEY DO NOTHING:

"We don't do it at all"

[2-sec Pause] That's totally fair...

Do you remember when you first made a decision about a product like ours?

[Time travel: roll back the clock to when they previously experienced pain]

OTHER - Latent Pain:

"We love Beta Corp mostly, but their Customer Service is pretty weak."

WHAT NOT TO DO:

"Our customer service is great. [Mary Poppins spoon-feed: Don't focus on YOUR solution yet!]"

WHAT TO DO:

"Oh, that's interesting; why is customer service important to you?" [Peel the onion]

"Well, as a matter of fact, our Customer Service team is based in Australia, so we need to wait one day to get a ticket answered. Not an issue except at the end of the month when we charge credit cards, customers can't refund for 72 hours & go ballistic"

"Oh no! What happens then?"

"It's costing us millions in negative Google reviews spilling blood on Page One."

"Oh, your customer service is an issue. What would happen if you fix it?"

"Honestly, I calculated we would reduce churn by 15%, adding 3 million in annual recurring revenue (ARR)."

[If they don't give you numbers, ask them to quantify opportunity cost.]

Step 4: Multiply

"Look, Nancy - don't change what you're currently doing (frictionless) - plug us in alongside Acme Corp to multiply the effectiveness of your current solution."

Other good action words for Multiply:

- Turbocharge
- Force multiplier
- Spike
- Boost

Remember "apathy is a convertible state."

Denial is the new status quo. We live in a world where you can offer a drowning human a lifeline, and they'll still adamantly argue that they don't need it.

My mentor, Tony J. Hughes, once told me: "Your greatest competitor is *do nothing*."

When you ask a prospect, "How's that working out for you?" They often say, "Fine" or "Meh, don't care - send info."

You need to "time travel" and ask them what was the use case or pain they originally solved when evaluating the incumbent solution. Triggering a past pain may put them back into that emotion and build up enough of a 'value gap' between their current solu-

123

tion, which hasn't completely done the job, and their expectations back then – which they've long forgotten about.

Then they can surface issues that you begin to peel. This technique is taken right out of the Freudian playbook in the "therapist" archetype, and it works.

MOVING ONTO VOICEMAILS: THE VOICEMAIL CONUNDRUM

Now that you understand how this method applies to cold calling, let's move on to voicemails.

Don't underestimate the power of a voicemail. Sure, it might initially feel awkward, but it serves a purpose.

Think of it this way, if you were out there knocking on doors to find prospects for a vacuum cleaner that can pick up a bowling ball, you would at least leave a flier behind to connect with anyone you might miss. You're not forcing these people to get in touch, but you are opening the door and giving them another opportunity to connect with you.

So, how do you make sure your voicemail resonates?

First, keep it short and sweet.

My voicemails are under a breath or two max. I never ask for a callback. I simply explain my reason for calling and that I'll follow up with a note.

The email follow-up always says, "Per my voicemail...." And that completes the *COMBO Prospecting* Triple - call, voicemail, and email in under 90 seconds flat.

Leaving 4-5 VMs produces callbacks - most sellers are terrified to go past 2 for fear of "lack of civility." The VM puts pressure on any digital channel to get an exponential response.

Drop slightly customized voicemails on all of your contacts in sequences. I call these "asynchronous doubles" or *async doubles*. (Call. Voicemail.) I can't stress how important it is to leave over three voicemails per prospect; this one factor alone has turned around failing reps.

Tenacity sends a signal to prospects: they can't help but react. Like the bill collector, they realize you're not going away. My most common response to extreme persistence is, "I'm so sorry," or even, "Jeeze, I should hire you to get some of that spirit around here – you remind me of *me* when I was your age."

Here's a voicemail template you can use inspired by Lee Bartlett:

> *"Hey Name, <REP NAME> from <COMPANY NAME>, <PHONE #>. I have a very relevant product to your work; do you mind if I tell you a bit about it? We have helped <RELEVANT LOGO> achieve <OUTCOME>. Again, <REP NAME> from <COMPANY NAME>, <PHONE #>. I'll follow up with a quick note. **[never ask for a call back]**"*

And here's an example:

> *"Hey Name, Justin Michael from Acme, 917.232.2164. I have a very relevant product to your work; do you mind if I tell you a bit about it? We have helped Acme, Beta, and Zeta drive a 46% increase in revenue via a single, unified platform for capital markets communication. Again, Justin Michael from Acme, 917.232.2164. I'll follow up with a quick note."*

As per the follow-up email, here's the template:

> *"Hey Name, per my voicemail, I have a product that's very relevant to your work; do you mind if I tell you a bit about*

it? We have helped <CASE STUDIES> achieve <OUTCOME>. Again, <REP NAME> from <COMPANY NAME>, <PHONE #>. If it makes sense to talk, how does your calendar look? [tap out]

And here's an example:

"Hey Name, Per my voicemail, I have a product that's very relevant to your work; do you mind if I tell you a bit about it? We have helped Acme, Beta, and Zeta drive a 46% revenue increase via a unified capital markets communication platform. If it makes sense to talk, how does your calendar look?"

Fun variant to the opener from Barrett Unger and Kellen Casebeer:

"Hey NAME - who at COMPANY is happiest when your yearly sales target gets hit?

It's hilarious how well it's been working for us - and here's why (I believe) it hits...

1. It's a fun question to answer. We transport them briefly to a world where they have succeeded in their yearly goal, and you tend to get a laugh or joking response back. AKA: prospects get a kick out of it.

2. It's a true pattern interrupt. This isn't your average SDR opener, and you will cause a legit pause from prospects as they ponder the question you just asked.

3. It's step one of Justin Michael's RRM cold call framework. We are essentially asking, "Who's the CEO of the problem?" which, in our case, means who owns hitting yearly sales targets (we are targeting Founders of smaller professional services businesses in this case).

126

They almost always answer, "Well, I do"...

4. We double down. The response to them usually isn't going into a pitch, but asking, "And are you more of a sports car kinda person, or a nice vacation type?"

Again - we are doubling the fun question // pattern interrupt, which also builds tremendous tension & curiosity in what you're calling about.

Deeper References: (Reach out for *Codex 7 & 13* on cold calling 3.0)

The first mind shift on a live call is to stop stealing the spotlight. Be *interested* instead of *interesting*.

When we fail to be curious, we miss our chance to flip the polarity as an unintended consequence. This happens involuntarily when we are relaxed, caring, and human, but sellers have amnesia. We forget to "sell without selling."

We can behave more naturally when we stop caring (too much) and detach from the outcome. Our brains tell us what to write, say, and do, just like when interacting with a trusted friend or colleague.

While you might never be able to stop caring as a salesperson, you can change what you focus your attention (caring) on. Care about the person you're speaking to and the outcomes they can achieve rather than the sale.

If you ever wonder, "Should I follow up?" Oops, you already should have. Err on the side of assertiveness, dare I say "aggression." Nature abhors a vacuum. Silence is not golden. For all the Jedi tactics I could teach you, what ultimately separates success and failure in sales, is simply a lack of follow-up.

Don't just work until you get the "yes." Work until you get the "no," too. A response - any response is the start of something. If you're not getting an answer, that's when you know you're not prospecting hard enough.

Be brave - bump it, and bump it again. Always add value. I challenge my clients, "See how many No's you can get this week."

Remember, Babe Ruth was the home run king and strike-out king. MTD Sales Training found that 80% of prospects say 'yes' after saying 'no' four times, but 92% of salespeople give up earlier. Frankly, I rarely even see two attempts. My CRO always loved me because I filled out our CRM's "notes/next steps" field. We knew where we stood in our market. I got an answer from every account - even if that answer was "no," "we use a competitor," or "2 quarters from now."

Whenever someone rejects a meeting, I'll use the Mike Weinberg classic VFV, "Why don't you visit with me anyway so we can see if there's a *fit* to drive *value*." So bold!

If you don't ask, you'll never get, as my Grandfather always said.

"91% of clients will give a referral, but only 11% of salespeople will ask for one." – Dale Carnegie

If your prospect rejects you twice, then ask for a referral.

Always get two "noes" and a referral. Put it on a Post-it note on your laptop. And be willing to launch a Hail Mary pass by bringing assumptive pains/challenges to them in the final seconds.

Prove your referrals with screenshots. Especially, if someone gives you a name in a LinkedIn message – take a screenshot as proof and email it to who you're referred to with the subject line: via Jane Smith. If you get a phone referral say, "I don't mean to be a sleazy salesperson; is it OK if I call Mike or perhaps you have his number?" "No, please don't mention my name but contact him." Get permission vs. just barrelling through calling Mike saying, "Jane said we should talk." They have Slack and will talk so don't ever lie or position it weirdly. Prospects love transparency and will help you.

Here's another tidbit that, if applied alone, would mint you into a millionaire. A multi-millionaire next-door insurance executive taught me this one.

My favorite way to ask for a referral is The Kindness Chain, "You're a nice person. Do you know any other nice people you can introduce me to?"

Sure, it sounds cheesy, but human beings love a little flattery. Admiration is scarce. If your prospect feels genuinely acknowledged and respected by you, the chances they'll want to help you skyrocket.

When you master the JMM, explode your funnel, or transform your consulting/coaching practice, you should raise rates and fire high-maintenance clients. Above all, work with friendly people like you who treat you with decorum, respect, class, and dignity. The secret to happiness is great clients.

Follow all these strategies, and eventually, you'll end up with a meeting on the books. That means you've won half the battle.

Now all you need to do is ensure they attend it. So, how do you do that?

I always send a calendar invite with an agenda missing the 4th topic to increase the likelihood. It looks like this:

Agenda:

    4) Your Company - Challenges & Objectives
    5) Our software - Tailored demo
    6) Q&A
    7) ?

Update the calendar invite two days before your meeting and ask, "Any agenda points you'd like to add?" This gives you an excuse to ping the entire thread and pressure test 'no-shows' to the meeting.

To close this section, I want to share an insight that humorously captures the ludicrous nature of this profession.

Justin Michael's first law: "No matter which outbound technique you use, if you set the meeting, you were right."

Changing the status quo is a massive element in the JMM, as is reverse psychology. If I could boil this entire system down into one phrase, it would be:

> *"Whatever you want to do, do the opposite. Whatever the prospect expects at that moment, do the opposite."*

> *"Whatever the majority of people are doing, under any given circumstances, if you do the exact opposite, you will probably never make another mistake as long as you live."*

> *– Earl Nightingale*

Nobody understands this better than Netflix. They end every damn episode in a cliffhanger, so we binge. We need to watch nine episodes to close a plot loop. From the first 10 minutes, we're hooked. So why not *cliffhanger* all our prospecting motions? This is especially useful for demos; share four if you have five awesome things to show. Hold something back for next time. The element of surprise!

Not only do invites without a message convert higher – because of mystery – cold calls that leave some mystery pique a reply.

Here's a mysterious voicemail template that you can use:

> *"Hey Name, I've got some ideas on how we could help you achieve <DESIRED OUTCOME> based on how we're helping <your largest competitor>. Let's find some time so I can share the why and the how. I'll follow up with a quick note."*

Of course, customize it more with elements from their business profile or google their name to "show 'em you know 'em," but don't spend more than 30 seconds doing this. The idea of 3X3 research – 3 personalization points in 3 minutes – needs to be 3 X 30 seconds. Scan and customize. Using quotes from articles or copying and pasting the exact recommendations from their profile works well. Just never fawn over them - instead: acknowledge, tailor, and customize to how your solution can help them without coming across like a stalker. Practice this skill, like speed reading.

To conclude this chapter, I want you to understand the first thing is and will always be your BEING. Who are you BEING when you ask for the business? Who are you TO THEM when you learn about their challenges?

Sometimes being direct and blunt is a superpower. Far too many people struggle with simply asking to form a business relationship. It is this gap that you want to learn to fill.

All the scripts in the world won't do anything if you don't fix this foundation first. In closing, the #10 employee at Marketo, now an SVP, says, "If you even try to call me, I'll book the meeting." That's how few people try to contact him.

Imagine we are both outrunning a bear, and you try to put on a pair of running shoes while I get on a Vespa. You'll get eaten! You only have to be a little bit better than the other 999 sellers attempting to reach your target, but this will have a far more potent effect on your success, helping you win by a country mile.

Do you want to practice your voicemails? At the end of leaving one, there's nearly always a set of options. Press the key to listen back, then re-record if you're unsatisfied. Do that 100 times and see just how good you get!

GPT Lab: practicing Cold Calling

A computer is a great listener.

Here are three prompts to help you practice your cold calling with a B2B buyer:

1. "You are a software buyer. Practice this role-play with me using this prompt. How can I grab your attention right off the bat and make you curious about my product?"
2. "What's a great way to break the ice and build rapport with a potential buyer over the phone?"
3. "How do I handle objections on a cold call without sounding pushy but still show them the value of my solution?"

OUTBOUND OBJECTION HANDLING

If you don't remove the obstacles to the sale, they cannot buy.

Objection handling is a huge deal in most training programs. Sales, and cold calling in particular, are whole institutions centered around objections. You'll handle a multitude of objections every day over the phone, email, and DM flows. Rejection is the cold, hard reality of life and especially of this job. But only by embracing failure, will you find your greatest success.

The JMM is about purposely provoking constant rejection, but knowing how to handle it like a pro. My favorite natural comparison for this is that of the honey badger. The honey badger is tough, it is strong, and it never gives up. Just as the honey badger takes a porcupine's quills and keeps on trucking, you must shake off or ignore an objection and keep on selling.

But unlike the honey badger, we cannot just blindly charge forward. We need to be more cunning, more cautious. Using rebuttals too fast and hard can make you seem defensive, especially in a chat flow. When you're chatting with people, mirror their speech pattern and pace of talking (beats per minute - BPM), to make your rebuttal part of the flow.

That is part of the Ack-Peel or "acknowledge peel" framework. You express you've heard someone or agree with them; then you attempt to peel the onion through questioning frameworks: things like SPIN, Challenger, running pain funnels, etc.

The biggest mistake in objection handling is failing to see the difference between an objection and a comment. The simplest form of this concept manifests in the most mundane of comments, such as, "I'm busy," or "I'm in a meeting right now." On the surface, these sound like solid attempts to brush you away with no further interaction. The experienced rep, however, sees this as a simple comment and asks, without skipping a beat, "No worries, shall I call you back at the top of the hour?" And remarkably, the prospect often says, "Sure," and even picks up.

"I'm on vacation" to the rookie rep becomes, "Oh sorry, I'll try you next week." The experienced rep jokes, "Oh nice, where are you at?" "The Bahamas, it's lovely," then proceeds with the call. What seems like a brush-off is actually further opportunity for discourse.

This brings me to the key objection handling heuristic of "humor diffusion."

Be humorous in a tasteful way - think Seinfeld vs. Chris Rock. Humor means different things to different people, so be aware of cultural sensitivities.

Below you'll find the responses to the top eleven cold-calling objections.

"I'm not interested"

How do you know you're not interested? I haven't even told you why I'm calling yet.

"I'll pass"

Hey, super quick favor: can you please coach me on how I could have made a better cold call? I just bombed!

"It's too expensive"

Relative to what ROI? We see 3-10X ROI on average. So it's a cash register versus a cost center. If you put 100K into a slot machine and got 300K, wouldn't you invest all day?

"Send me some information"

I could do that, but this will blow your mind; every time in my career I send info, it goes into the circular file. Are you really just telling me I'll never talk to you again? Admit it!

"We don't have any budget left"

That's fine, what about pulling from a lateral budget, like Marketing? [insert function]

"We have that covered / All set / We have everything we need"

Oh, excellent, I make these calls all day. Can you tell me how you've managed to solve this? Because most people I call are struggling.

"I'm not responsible for that"

No worries, who's the appropriate person to reach out to? Would you be up to making a warm intro?

"We have a vendor"

I get it, most of our customers were with another vendor, but when they saw how our solution could augment/turbocharge their existing stack, they plugged us in alongside it any way to multiply the effectiveness — MULTIPLY (from RRM). Or, if they name them: they're great, how's it working out for you?

"This isn't a priority now"

1. I get it; it could be high urgency in another quarter. What would make it a priority for you?

2. Can you walk me through your current focus, and I can help you with that?

"It's confidential"

That's fine; I assume it's [massive competitor or "a state secret."] They're great — how's it working out for you? [assumptive RUIN]

"I'd never take a cold call"

Wait, you're running [sales/marketing/revenue], and you won't take calls? Aren't I doing exactly the best practice you want your people to do? [Challenger]

For a breakdown of the 50 top HubSpot rebuttals and how to handle them with Ack-Peel and Humor Diffusion, see *Codex 14*.

When it comes to budding sales reps, I'm constantly asked, "What's the best way to get past gatekeepers?"

My best answer is: "treat them like gold; just like your champion in a matrixed account." Ask them, "Hey, can I pitch you on what I want to show Jane?" Or, handle the resistance constructively saying, "Hey, I know this is the 200th vendor call you got today; if I really wanted to get a message to Rick, how would I do it?" It creates a pattern interrupt if you level with them or appeal to their logic and power. When confronted by objections, try to see if they'll help you on the merits of your tech vs. brushing past them fast or getting dropped into voicemail boxes. I've had entire board meetings set by Executive Assistants that I won over.

You better get used to "navigated dials" if you want to win big in an era where cold calling has been falsely pronounced dead. Knowing how to traverse the winding streets of an automated switchboard will be vital in getting yourself heard by the people who matter to you.

In other cases you will find yourself on call with a real-life switch-board operator. Dealing with these flesh-and-blood prospects is more challenging. There are many ways that you can find yourself brushed off before you even get the chance to speak to anyone else. In these cases it helps to know who you're after. Just say the full name with a downtone like you own the place and they'll pass you right through, Obi-Wan. After all, 50% of meetings are coming from "conversations that required a human to navigate" according to Gerry Hill & ConnectAndSell looking at a slice of 10MM calls over the last 2 years (out of 150MM B2B dials.)

Now, let's get you to send response-triggering emails.

GPT Lab: Objection Handling

GPT knows objections.

Here are a few prompts to help you respond to typical B2B buyer objections:

1. "You are a buyer of my B2B/B2C product. How do I ease your concerns about the price of my product without devaluing it or giving in too easily?"
2. "What's a convincing way to show buyers my solution is better than what they're currently using or considering?"
3. "How can I effectively address a buyer's worry about my product's implementation and integration process?"

Cold Email Copywriting

"I read this section of the JMM and shared it with my team. Within 100 sends without even perfect email data, we set 7 appointments on the first message."

- Daniel Wax, CRO, SelfDisrupt

Even if you're a trained copywriter, you may still be getting your emails wrong.

Because what you put into a B2B cold email is distinctively different to what you write in a marketing message. You must rewire yourself to write as you speak, conversationally, in broken sentences, what I like to call: grammar funk.

No more paragraphs! I know it's heretical. Think of your initial emails like creating a "business haiku." Short, broken sentences. Waste no time in the first 18 words from the subject line to preview text. Essentially, put the whole email in the subject line.

I call emails in the JMM – "SPEARS" – because they're laser-focused, short, to the point, and blunt. Here's one way to build one:

"SPEARS"

Subject line: <relevant info bit> + <key word>

Greeting: Hey <<name>>

Sentence 1: <<mention relevant info bit>>, curious if you're open to discuss <<specific outcome related to key word>> strategy?

Sentence 2: <<lookalike customer>> uses us to <<achievable outcome>> by (x% or $x).

CTA: If it makes sense, when can we hop on a zoom?

Think of your cold email like a tweet: Short, one-lined statements, compacted to allow no paragraph breaks:

Hey Brian – Based on how we helped [similar company to them] achieve [awesome super power thing only HubSpot does] to get [this amazing quantifiable result], there's a lot we could be doing w/ your Co. - up for a chat?

The bellwether of strong cold email copywriting is if it will hold up on a smartphone when you send it to yourself, friends, peers, and colleagues. For a greater sense of how effective your work is, include people that aren't directly involved in the project. The wisdom of crowds is powerful, and even the very book in your hands was heavily edited based on initial feedback from hundreds of voices, much like screening a movie to a test audience.

Remember: A/B test everything. Think in micro, not just macro.

Copywriting for B2B is an exercise in brevity, short-form content of three sentences or less, and soft calls-to-action. It's not a place for 3 paragraph expository essays that trigger a "fight or flight" reaction in executive prospects' brains as they frantically stare at it in Gmail, or inevitably abandon it. Here are some principles I retrained traditional copywriters with when scaling an agency to 100 concurrent clients, writing all their messaging for them, and generating thousands of meetings.

TOP TEN RULES OF B2B EMAIL COPYWRITING

1. Write an email you can read in 3 seconds. For added restraint: tap it out with your thumbs on a mobile device, and once done: "Kill a word," à la Aaron Ross.
2. Optimize the subject line (3 words max) and preview text (only shows ±18 words). Get sharp and noticeable, think modern art: Picasso meets Miró. Examples: "Name X reduce risk," "Company + 367%," "Attack Surfaces" (weird one from cyber security)
3. Think of Seth Godin's purple cow: "What's going to make this stand out?" If possible, add in:
   - A joke
   - An image
   - A GIF
   - A weird word or symbol
4. What's in it for the prospect? Immediately get into social proof - companies care about results: who you help, similar to them. Build a list of approved name drops by vertical with pocket stories. Make sure you limit any "I statements" in emails; instead use "you." "I, me, or mine" will kill a conversion.
5. Be specific, not vague, to keep yourself sounding as legitimate as you are. Avoid anything that looks like a false claim (e.g.,

round numbers like 100% vs. 97.34%). Any benefits must be quantified!

6. Remember Steve Richard's four demand types: make money, save money, reduce risk, and satisfy government regulation.

    a. The most important two are regulation and risk, in that order. "We have a product that prevents GDPR violations." "We can mitigate your risk of breach."

    b. I also love a 5th: solve an irritation: the DocuSign example: no more print cartridges or flatbed scanner hell!

7. Per Tony Robbins, humans move away from fear (risk/loss aversion) vs. toward pleasure, so flip your emails. Instead of, "Look at all this money you could make," lace it with fear-based innuendo: "Imagine the opportunity cost of losing millions not patching this security hole." The vast majority of emails I read lose their message because they are too positive and jeopardize their impact. Add FUD: fear, uncertainty, and doubt!

8. Speak in the conversational language of your prospects. Make it a B2B mullet: business in the front, party in the back. Use the Hemingway app to dumb it down to a 5th-grade reading level (low Flesch–Kincaid score). Write like you talk where you talk like you know them.

9. Industry jargon can help you if it displays acumen, e.g., Logistics or Trucking SaaS, and terms native to those professions. Technojargon looks snobby and turns off prospects.

10. Per Tony J. Hughes, C-Level executives speak the language of "outcomes and risk," so you'll need gravitas (carry yourself powerfully), acumen (deep business model knowledge), and

savvy (wisdom of knowing use cases and value drivers) to cut through.

I took journalism for a semester and leveraged the journalistic approach to create the ideal starting point for what would become my cold email mantra to this day.

The purpose of the subject line is to get the first sentence read. The purpose of the opening sentence is to get the 2nd sentence read. The goal of the body of the email is to get the CTA read and inspire the recipient to respond. That's like Todd Caponi's Yogi Berraism, "The purpose of any step in the sales process is to... wait for it... drumroll, please. GET TO THE NEXT ONE!" The ideal email (or call) should have a cascade effect that draws the reader in and carries them gently towards our goal - a meeting.

One visual trick I use within cold emails is to highlight a CTA with neon yellow (or blue) like an actual highlighter pen which pulls the eye to anywhere I want in a proposal or email.

Justin Michael (thejmike@gmail.com)

thoughts?

Hey Doug, Based on how we're helping Beta, Alpha, and Omega reduce ad fraud by 43% with our proprietary data science LLMs, we could be doing a lot with Your Co. up for a chat?

--
Justin Michael
Executive Coach & Bestselling Author
TechPoweredSalesBook.com

Justin Michael Method email example

The concept almost writes itself in its simplicity, but here's another great exercise to create awesome cold emails in seconds.

Imagine that you're riding in an elevator in Manhattan, and Mark Cuban steps in. You've got until the ground floor to impress him. He's heard every last possible pitch. What would you say?

1. What's in it for him? (WIIFM) How can he make money, save money, or reduce risk?
2. What's different about your product that he hasn't seen/ heard before? (think purple cow)
3. What specific, quantified social proof do you have from other companies that wouldn't necessarily impress him but would build authority?
4. Remember the Mark Cuban Test: what's your unfair competitive advantage, is it defensible, and are YOU credible to execute it?

Don't waste time giving in to your admiration. Yes, we respect him, but you notice that I didn't fawn over him, or let myself be distracted from my goal. No doubt he hears such praise as "Oh, I love your work on Shark Tank. Go, Mavs!" a thousand times a day. You need to take a page out of his book and put aside your feelings for your cause, because senior executives have seven slots in their mind, per Mike Bosworth. They are laser-focused on only these priorities and challenges. So you need to speak to a burning desire or pain and be hyper-brief.

Example of what to say to him:

"Hey Mark, I've developed a neuroscience-backed method to train sales reps that 2-5Xs their pipeline, but what's unique is emails look like text messages and ad units, and I send visual Venn diagrams. It shot the lights out at Salesforce, HubSpot, and LivePerson. Perhaps I could dramatically move the needle in a few of your portfolio companies?"

Ground floor. Game. Set. Match. Ya dig?

I ran this approach by VC Doug Landis once, and he corrected me, "Or, you could just tell a compelling story." He's right!

There are various tools at this writing that inject ChatGPT, and you should leverage this to enhance outbound emails. As you write, the tech can make them more persuasive and assertive, add in empathy, or shorten/simplify. All these minor edits stack the deck in your favor to get the result you want, whether that's a warm response or ultimately closing the deal. If you're struggling to trim down your writing yourself, seek tools such as:

- GrammarlyGO (generative AI)
- Regie.ai (GPT sequence injection)
- Autobound.ai (hyper-personalize emails in seconds)
- Lavender.ai (sales email coach)
- Substrata.me for dealmakers (social signal processing - behavioral intelligence) – *Substrata's Adaptive AI is designed to decode implicit human dynamics, understanding both .semantics and the often overlooked subtleties of non-verbal communication. At its core, Substrata reads and predicts the perceptions, feelings, and attitudes of potential clients. This unique ability fast-tracks deal negotiations, and provides an unusual competitive edge to any dealmaker.*

The biggest paradox I've found in my work testing millions of emails is: personalization to the person decreases results. Green reps write bad emails, so the personalization makes them *marginally* better and lifts conversion metrics. Experienced reps trigger pain/latent pain, leverage use cases, and are assumptive in implications plus ROI business case imputed, taking a trusted advisor approach to align with critical concerns of C-Levels.

I've never met a C-Level who wanted to meet with me because we discovered we both like Miles Davis. Have you? The Kyle Coleman approach of the "handsome emails" gets praise from the low-level responder here and there but the higher you aim, the less you should pander.

My emails have been called "ugly" and "awkward." But they slaughter the "beautiful" ones. Keep it short; make it uglier. As an amusing aside, I've been working with Soham Sarkar & another client in biotech to get GPT to do "ugly." So far: it can't.

Only humans can hold an ugly sweater contest, for now. Your 10th-grade English teacher and CMO may revolt, but that 60% open rate and 3-5% conversion rate tastes sweet.

Let's dive into six advanced email tips and examples:

TIP 1: ANALYZING WEBSITES

Find something broken or suboptimal on a landing page, form fill, etc. Or, find a negative review on a review site. Screenshot it in your email as one of the core problems you can fix. Poke the wound, twist the knife, and only then, use your pitch to bandage it.

TIP 2: USE VIDEO

Use a Vidyard or Loom video email to show your HubSpot dashboard with complete analytics on the integration they could see. (If you do use link outs, keep them short for deliverability). Create a use case fly through (with your head in the lower corner). Remember: diagnose & prescribe. HubSpot has an awesome use case library by metric. Another trick is if you don't have a case study in a vertical like Beauty/Cosmetics but you know they monetize on site conversions and email nurture, show a business outcome from another vertical in E-Commerce even Sporting Goods that has the same funnels and monetization flow. Use case selling is massive and you can close a 7-figure enterprise deal off just one like instant mobile surveys for an airline.

TIP 3: MYSTERY SHOP

Pretend you're their customer. Submit a lead request on their site. Time how fast you get a call back to gauge "speed to lead." If something is broken or delayed there, it's the kind of thing that will immediately land a meeting with a CEO or CMO.

TIP 4: FLIP FROM GAIN TO PAIN

Rewrite any email with a positive message displayed negative. Example FOMO: "You could increase revenue by 23%," becomes, "You could be missing out on 77% of potential revenue."

TIP 5: REWORK YOUR BUMPS

Bumps should be lowercase and no signature: "thoughts?"

(Side note: place your opt-out as a P.S. on touch 1 and 3, "P.S. Let me know if you'd like to stop getting these." The hard coded links are spammy by default so turn them off for better deliverability.)

TIP 6: USE AI TO SHORTEN EMAILS

GrammarlyGO has a great ChatGPT email shortener to hone in on an optimal SPEAR leveraging JMM heuristics.

JMM Sequence Mastery

In 2017, I became the VP of Ops in a Silicon Valley startup, fully automating the top funnel and helping scale it to 100 concurrent tech customers, acquiring an AI-personalization "sentence injection engine" maxing out Outreach.io's custom fields. After 15 years in the mobile marketing industry, my first move to optimize client messaging was brevity.

This simple tweak later formed the bedrock of JMM-style messaging in any medium. Nearly every B2B trainer has changed their stance from long to short form. That should tell you everything you need to know.

We sent millions of emails in the startup, and found compacting all messaging down to under 50 words (3 sentences max) saw an immediate spike in campaign 'open rates' to 60-80%. F-Curve eye tracking is a myth. If there's enough text for that, you've already failed. Think about it, under 50 words is 2.5 sentences. So F-Curve your landing pages, sure. It's very 2015 thinking!

The second innovation was in the rhythm (or cadence) of the sequence sending itself. Believe it or not, I might be the first person in B2B history to suggest sending assertive messages on Day 2.

In the past, most sequences and cadences were run on Day 1, Day 3, and Day 5. The Agoge Sequence from 2017 is safe and expected.

Virtually every company uses this method. Again, anything that becomes too popular becomes expected. The JMM will stay valid like Madonna because once the entire industry is using it, you can simply flank a heuristic. If everyone is short, go long.

Test new frequencies, message length, blended combinations, and challenge conventional syntax (even in 2100 CE).

It's time for sellers to stop trying to sneak into the inboxes of decision makers. Be bold and open with your intention to set meetings.

The right number of messages, sent at the right times, conveys a subliminal signal to a prospect's subconscious mind that they need to respond, a concept Craig Elias described as "selective awareness." It's a different approach to your typical "slow-rolled" sequenced emails that softly drizzle their way over 4-6 weeks.

C-Levels know what they want. If you are aggressive enough in getting a message in front of them, the reply coming back on day two vs. day 62 is nearly always the same. If they're going to say "no" on day 62, they can say it on day 2 as well.

Day 1 message, Day 2 bump, Day 3 visual, rest day 4. It's a geometric shape that repeats. Each message *cluster* has its own narrative arc.

Who would posit making over seven touches in the first 24 hours without risking a restraining order? I ended up calling this digital blitzkrieg "bee swarming."

The next cluster hits symmetrically on Day 5 with a new message, Day 6 as a bump, and Day 7 as a visual (Venn, GIF, etc.) Interlace each cluster with a "narrative arc." So Cluster 1 gets a universal value prop, Cluster 2 testimonials, Cluster 3 use cases, and Cluster 4 G2 Crowd reviews/grids in no particular order. Improvise your heart out!

This sequence architecture gave rise to the hotly contested "thoughts?" bump on day 2. And these bumps became GIFs, emojis, and myriad hilarious iterations. My favorites are the Clooney Bump, where he's popping his head over the Hawaiian golf course hill, and the Batman Bump, which flashes the bat signal with the word "thoughts?" inside. But I also like sending a golfer & golf tee emoji, or just a subtle cloud emoji with a crystal ball for "thoughts."

Leading software companies think they debunked the "thoughts bump" theory with research. But my clients still hit it out of the park on Day 2 every day. Why?

Because the first message is so irresistible. If you bump garbage, of course, you'll get crickets (which threw off the analysts). It also works to send "thoughts?" to any dormant email reply where you've been ghosted, regardless of the time delay since that reply. Mario Krivokapic writes: "Any movement on this?" OR, "Any merit in this?" both convert very well as alternates.

Remember, it's a heuristic (linguistic shortcut).

Create bursts of messages that fire daily, building message threads. Your clusters should be composed of one subject line and subsequent messages that "bump up" to the top of the inbox list. This catches the prospect's eye in an Outlook or GMail inbox from a mobile or web browser.

Here's the complete 2020's sequence structure that flies in the face of The Agoge Sequence by Sam Nelson:

THE JMM SEQUENCE

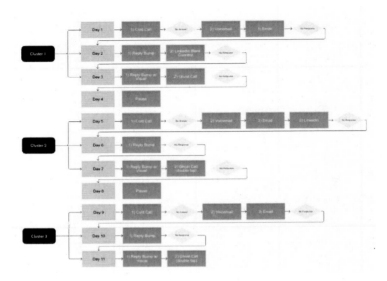

Mind map of the JMM Sequence

Cluster #1

Day 1: Call, VM, Email (Triple)
Day 2: Re: Email 1 (Reply Bump), LinkedIn blank connect ("mystery" connect - creates intrigue)
Day 3: Reply bump with a visual, ghost call (call w/o leaving a VM)

Cluster #2

Day 5: (Triple), LinkedIn
Day 6: (Reply Bump)
Day 7: (Reply Bump), ghost call (or double tap)

Cluster #3

Day 9: (Triple)
Day 10: (Reply Bump)

Day 11: (Reply Bump), ghost call (or double tap)

Clusters and Narrative Arcs - email thread architecture:

((You could extend the sequence shape like this / give context))
{cluster1 – universal narrative/unique value proposition}
Day 1
Day 2
Day 3
Rest

{cluster2 – case study related to vertical/use case}

Day 5
Day 6
Day 7
Rest

{cluster3 – testimonials / G2 crowd review or grid screenshot}

Day 9
Day 10
Day 11
Rest

Day 13 breakup

You could always add one more cluster. The general idea is to bring potentially different narratives into Cluster 2 and Cluster 3, such as:

- Case studies
- G2 crowd grid (screenshot)
- Customer quotes/stories
- Use cases

Side note: Notice the geometry of the JMM sequence. It's fractal holographic. Every touch point can stand alone as an outreach instead of referring to an email four days ago. "Did you read the PDF I sent?" is not a hologram or fractal. It makes customers work. They need to dig through past emails, looking for pertinent tidbits. Ensure every thread can stand alone to fully convert from a holistic messaging perspective.

Below is the ENTIRE template you can steal to use on your own.

Before diving into the clusters, remember that you can use different variations for the subject line. Subject line generation is a top use case for ChatGPT because it really gets us out of the white space frustration of sourcing new ideas. I'll cover that a little more later in the book... Find some strong options below:

1. Triplet, in two forms:
    a. Last unrelated topic - "growth, 2023, F1"
    b. Curiosity-driving words - SLA, 37, [Company name]
        i. You can extract these directly from the email
2. [uncommon commonality] - "triathlon race"
3. [Pain point]? - "anemic pipeline?"
4. [Emotion] this? - "hate this"?
    a. You can use triggering verbs like 'despise,' 'hate,' 'love,' etc.
5. [jobs to be done] - "running monthly payouts"
6. via [connection] - "via Mark Wahlberg"
7. Open loop - "used RRM to close 37 deals in a row"

Cluster #1

Day 1: Email 1

Subj: [template] ex: growth

Hey {{first_name}} -- curious if you're open to chat re: [blank] strategy? [Customer] achieved [outcome] in [timeframe] with us by [process]. If it makes sense, should we set up some time to chat? Thanks -JWD John Denver / Company / ### ### ####

Day 2: Bump #1

Hey {{first_name}} - any thoughts? or, just lowercase: thoughts?

Day 3: Bump #2

What do you think are the implications of this diagram? [insert Venn diagram w/ opinion heuristic]

Venn Diagram example

Cluster #2

Day 5: Email #2

Subj: [template] ex: innovation

Hey {{first_name]} - any initiatives to allocate budget towards [blank] in 2022? I have a product that may be able to [reduce risk, reduce spend, increase revenue, etc.] -- [pain point]. If this is on your radar, should we set something up for Q4? Thanks -JWD

Day 6: Bump #1

[Relevant customer quote]

Day 7: Bump #2

[visual, case study, screenshot, etc.]

Cluster #3

Day 9: Email 3

Subj: [template] ex: reduce risk

Hey (FirstName]] Have you heard [current event] [pain point]? What steps are you taking to ensure your bases are covered? P.S. Would love to show some of the recent work we've done for companies to avoid these situations. Lemmeno

Day 10: Bump #1

[gif/video] - Recommended gif creators: Zight or Gyazo.com

Day 11: Bump #2

[customer quote]

Here are a few things you need to keep in mind when working with clusters:

1. Swap out the use cases you highlight by persona and run 3-5 contacts per account.
2. If they don't respond in 10 business days, run 2 more clusters, emails bumped twice each, drop a "break up," then swap out for another contact.

Soft calls-to-action (CTAs) & Safe words:

These are my favorite calls to action, all interest-based. Never ask for 15-30 minutes of their time again! Once I asked for 12 minutes, the prospect jokingly agreed to give me 11. So I said, "OK, I'll bring my stopwatch."

1) If it makes sense to talk, how does your calendar look?
2) When's a good time to talk?
3) Up for a quick Zoom? or, Up for a chat? or, worth exploring? (try 'em lowercase, even w/ spelling mistakes or swear words to increase performance per Gong.io)
4) Talk soon (highest sign-off performer according to Jeremey Donovan)

Remember - keep it to a single question per email. This is the David Ogilvy original "Mad Man" one-word brand equity concept. Starbucks = coffee.

Ideally, each "spear" should contain only one idea, thought, or referenced brand and no more than one question. Need to say more? Use a reply bump.

Salesloft has found that one question, and only one, has on average a better reply rate (+7%) than none at all. The more questions, the worse it gets (-8.4% with two, -19.1% with 3 and -39.1% with 4).

Also, use pattern interrupts amply, even punctuation or syntax: use a period where you'd naturally put a question mark. It conveys confidence and a down tone vs. an up tone.

I'll credit the legendary Tom Hopkins with my thoughts on "safe words." Bryan Kreuzberger influenced my thinking here greatly, too. Consider the difference between an unsafe word like "religion" and its safe counterpart, "philosophy."

1) Don't say "contract," say "agreement."
2) Don't say "schedule," say "calendar."
3) Don't say "love" (super needy); say "I'd welcome the opportunity to meet."

See my point?

We drove thousands of meetings for 100+ concurrent clients with this structure to scale OutboundWorks. Don't judge my email systems with vanity metrics, test them for yourself.

Remember, even if your open rates and reply rates go down, but the caliber of the prospects you connect with increases, you'll land much bigger deals. The hardest-to-reach budget holders don't sit around complimenting vendor emails. They only respond to laser-focused *relevance* that hits a pain or latent pain.

Plus, open rates are now just a proxy after Apple shifted its iPhone pixel tracking settings allowing all users to block it hard.

The JMM uniquely produces meetings with the highest quality prospects, not just more appointments—a fundamental distinction.

How do you write killer emails every time? You run them through the top ten heuristics:

1. Brevity
2. Specificity
3. Social proof
4. Differentiated value prop (IP)
5. Fear/pain emotional resonance (use Plutchik's 'Wheel of Emotion')
6. Storytelling
7. Soft CTA
8. Tap out
9. BS alarm
10. Scarcity

    ... you can come up with them endlessly

Heuristics are mental shortcuts or linguistic meta-frameworks/ formulas for maximizing results with neuroscience.

There aren't just 10. You can iterate on them infinitely. Hat tip to the exceptionally researched work of David Hoffeld.

By the way, "BS Alarm" is an action step.

Scarcity creates value. Limitation/exclusivity creates value. Think about it. If everyone had a Ferrari, would you still want one?

"The swagger breeds." - Jim Mongillo

Test your emails on the BS alarms of your colleagues, friends, and loved ones to see if they "call BS." Your messages should make perfect sense from the preview text on mobile before the click. People whose opinion you respect should see them and say, "I would click." The holy grail is writing a subject line so good, they hit reply without even opening your email. That's like hitting a hole-in-one in golf but I have done it.

Emails that are three sentences long take the brain 3.3 seconds to process. Emails that are three paragraphs trigger the "fight or flight" reflex in the amygdala (older lizard brain) and take 11 seconds to read.

C-Levels will think your long email is a bill, tax info, or lawsuit. They'll star or flag the email and never come back. Who has the time?

Stop subconsciously triggering them incorrectly and instead leverage hyper-short, conversational messages to draw them near.

A game of heuristics is never zero-sum. Instead of sending the same template like everyone else does, dismantle an email template that conforms well to heuristics along these lines:

Hey {{Name}}

– Lack of pleasantry

– Social proof

– Case study ref

– Ref X, Y, Z, Quantitative Benefit

Example: "Hey Jane, We helped Acme get a 46% margin increase with logistics automation. The VP of Supply Chain went from overwhelmed to relieved as she could finally track the root causes delaying shipping w/ our advanced algorithms to display analytics, giving full visibility. up for a zoom?"

This is meta. This is a framework.

Hey {{Name}}

– Humor opener

– Common connection-specific

– Braun Illumination question (imagine if you could do ___ amazing thing: superpower vs. sword__?)

– Gratitude

Example: "Hey Jane, My AI broke, and somehow this personalized email slipped through. Looks like we both know Max Altschuler (but I actually know him for real). Imagine if you could visualize your entire supply chain with AI-enabled analytics. MAERSK put in our new system to see a 46% margin increase on its shipping container line of business (LOB). Thanks, JM"

Here's some of the best advice I can give you on writing sequences: Think in fractals and holograms. In these systems, any one part is equal to the whole. Fractals repeat themselves as you zoom in.

The Mandelbrot set is a clear example of fractals at work. It's generated by iteration, which means repeating a process repeatedly. The functions involved are called quadratic polynomials and have the form:

$$f(x) = ax^2 + bx + c$$

Where c is a constant number.

In plain English, the shape repeats infinitely as you zoom in. The JMM geometry is a tribute to mathematician Benoit Mandelbrot. The Mandelbrot set was called "fingerprints of God" by Arthur C. Clarke, who inspired "Blade Runner," my favorite movie ever! Fractals are also the hallmark of my work to honor my grandfather, a nuclear physicist who ran a particle accelerator with isotope discoveries to his credit.

What are the implications of mathematics on outbound prospecting? Simply put, it means writing email 11, so it holds up against the whole sequence of 27 touches intrinsically.

Never guilt the prospect. Never remind them you are soliciting. Never ask why they haven't been responding. Never prompt them to click a link, watch something outside of what plays in line, and don't bore them to tears with PDFs.

Read the PDF yourself and pull out the top salient point to include in the body copy of a touch. Hilariously, a VP I know, used to send photos of himself crying in a suit or banging his head against a keyboard. Not a good look. Extra-needy repellant.

To conclude this chapter, two subject matter experts share their insights on cold email.

Per RevOps expert Jeff Ignacio:

> *"There is an art to writing cadences. Like anything, using old-hat techniques loses its effect over time. A diminishing marginal benefit as the 'same' playbook, message schema, or headline comes across the airwaves. I'd argue to start with developing what outcomes you're trying to drive, then developing strategies/plays that could hit those outcomes. Release. Then tweak along the way in cohorts holding all things constant except one variable. Then proceed to the next cohort."*

Deon Don, my Ops lead at OutboundWorks, contributes:

> *"Cooks follow Recipes. Chefs understand the principles of food so that they can tweak and invent. See yourself as the master chef who infinitely tweaks the burger. The burger*

is always changing. To the eater, it always tastes delicious, but they don't know why.

You must extract the recipe from the finished dish. Following the recipes you created, one must be aware of deep context (the hologram). Ultimately, we are talking to both chefs and cooks simultaneously."

DE-THREADING

I invented this term because it describes breaking an email chain to follow up with each stakeholder individually after a critical meeting or demo call to sleuth what's happening in the account.

If you endlessly "check in" on the main thread, you might not realize that the CEO of the Problem is out sick with COVID or on vacation in Thailand.

In the old days of strategic selling, we'd "pre-wire" a big meeting by calling each stakeholder in advance and asking what they wanted to cover. That's pretty hard to do now.

Therefore, you need to de-thread after a big meeting and write a message leveraging an "opinion heuristic" to each stakeholder asking:

"What did you get out of that presentation? Anything I missed or could have improved? What was your candid opinion of it?"

This is where you'll uncover hidden data points, competitive vendors in the deal, and validate decision makers. Maybe someone is unhappy or traveling, and you don't know it yet. So don't just leave four people on the thread and keep pinging the main chain every two weeks until they throw up their hands and tell you, "We'll pass."

With all prospecting, there is a decay rate similar to Steve Chandler's "half-life of enthusiasm." In other words, we must strike when the iron is hot.

Immediate, relevant follow-up keeps the convo going in threads, WhatsApp messages, DMs, SMS, and calls.

WhatsApp Theory: The more humans you have access to in real-time = the more income.

Interactivity = close rate.

The best salespeople are in near-constant communication with prospective buyers. I co-manage multiple mastermind groups this way across dark social (WhatsApp, Slack, Discord), and all my clientele is working with me in real time. Deals close 10X faster and issues resolve at 100X the speed of waiting on emails.

My clients succeed because they sell to the customer in their own words.

The insights a prospect shares in discovery calls are leveraged to create future conversations and demos.

Revelations from the first meeting get played back bespoke to each person. For instance, "Jane, in our meeting, you mentioned that X was a priority for you. I've attached this case study highlighting how we can help you achieve Y business outcome specifically." Or, "Per your request, here's the analysis of that implementation you were interested in seeing." Intel is another reason getting a mutual non-disclosure agreement (MNDA) in place before the first call is mission-critical.

The lack of tailoring and customization in most sales processes is astounding. Be 1% better in your messaging and outrun 99% of your competitors.

INTRO PROOF

Trust is at an all-time low nowadays, so you must make minor tweaks when referred; you'll be surprised how many salespeople simply lie.

First, whenever someone forwards your email, write back to that person, "Once we talk, I'll report back." Then, flip the email to whom you're referred, changing the subject line from "FWD:" to "RE:," which will create more mystery-proof and increase your reply rate. This is a direct Bryan Kreuzberger-inspired technique.

Second, whenever you receive a referral on LinkedIn, screenshot it as "proof" and put it "inline" into an email with the subject line, "Via <FULL NAME of the referrer>." Again, it proves a bonafide referral happened.

During the sales process, stay in touch with the referrer to help you close the deal, creating a three-way referral flywheel. Sellers always leave the referrer for dead when that influential person could help set a meeting or close a deal. Reward the referrer with a book, offer to write them a recommendation, find out how you can *serve* them. Even offer 20%!

A corollary to this idea is cross-referencing channels. Sometimes the fastest way to get an email response is to write this simple spear on LinkedIn x-ref'd: "I've been trying to get ahold of you by email." Suddenly, you'll get a reply from their email address after they finally go and check. This leverages the same principle as leaving a VM to increase response rates on inmail/emails.

BREAK UP EMAILS

Instead of a magic bullet script for this, I think about Robert Cialdini's concepts of "congruence," "consistency," and "liking" to come up with something that sounds like this hat tip by Maurice Kelter at HubSpot Oz.

"My previous emails have yielded no return; let me explain why I'm reaching out to you. [drop a personalized video]"

The other last-ditch email I love comes from Sean G. Cook from my Salesforce ExactTarget days. The word courtesy is such a trigger. We all have been raised to be courteous and must be congruent or consistent with this value:

Can you please have the courtesy to point me in the right direction to who handles this?

A couple of funnier breakup email variants leveraging the humor heuristic are as follows:

"Name, my attempts to catch you have yielded no response. I wrote a song about it. Can I get your thoughts? [Paste Justin Bieber lyrics to "What Do You Mean."] What's crazy is that a rep quit a FinTech role in Manhattan, sent the Bieber Lyrics on his last day, and closed a 6-figure deal inadvertently. Unreal! The other one is a revamp of those mid-2000s multiple-choice breakup lists but satirized.

Name, you are not responding to my elegant outreach sequence, so i'm guessing:

    a.   You were eaten by an alligator

    b.   An armoire fell on you

    c.   I need to put you on a milk carton

d.   All of the above?

Luke Marlowe had a cool idea to get a VA to scrape the customer logos on each prospect's website and then refer to them in the email. "Wouldn't you like to get more customers like Alpha, Beta, & Zeta?"

He did something similar by scraping the top 3 reps on a prospect's sales team and saying, "What if we could feed better leads to Suzy, Gerry, and Kevin?" Customization like this will make you stand out from the crowd.

Again, the more human your prospect believes you to be, the better. Personalization helps you build rapport more than anything else.

Last but not least, I'd like to pay tribute to Josh Braun for coming up with a highly effective way to trigger a response. Here's the template below:

Subject line: Apology

Body:

{{firstName}},

Please accept my apology.

It looks like somewhere along the line, I did a poor job of explaining how <YOUR COMPANY> could help with <OUT-COME>.

My intent isn't to move forward. Just wondering if you'd be open to sharing some feedback so I could better address your needs in the future?

Timing off? Money? Humor-based question?

Okay, hopefully, that wasn't too painful. Thanks for reading. Either way, all the best for the coming months.

And here's an example below:

Subject line: Apology

Body:

John,

Please accept my apology.

It looks like somewhere along the line, I did a poor job of explaining how our SDR team could help you book 15-20 more sales meetings this month.

My intent isn't to move forward. Just wondering if you'd be open to sharing some feedback so I could better address your needs in the future?

Timing off? Money? Don't trust bald men?

Okay, hopefully, that wasn't too painful. Thanks for reading. Either way, all the best for the coming months.

Why does it work?

First, people don't want to feel like they've been an asshole to you, hence the apology.

Then, you are restating the desired outcome, detaching from the close (my intent isn't to move forward), and asking for feedback in a humble way.

You close off with a humor trifecta, and a sentence: "hopefully that wasn't too painful" to increase the reply rate.

Icing on the cake: you genuinely wish them good things, which never hurts.

Send this, and you'll be back in the game most of the time, with the prospect sharing their concerns and potential objections.

No case studies? No problem

Sometimes you have to hit the ground running from a cold start.

Obviously, testimonials, case studies, and customer hero stories are all valuable tools in your sales arsenal. If you don't have these resources already, it might be worth doing some free pilots or proof of concepts to expand your toolkit.

But let's say, for now, you don't have any quantified metrics or social proof to refer to when writing sequences. In that case, your best bet is to leverage an incendiary news story to create intrigue. Or you can draw attention to how others in your space are solving common issues to create a compelling pain/solution story frame.

For example, I once worked with a cybersecurity anti-fraud technology company in Australia. They couldn't share their case studies due to strict privacy controls, but they found other ways to boost engagement:

> *"Did you notice the poultry breach that happened recently and caused $2MM in losses because their firewall and back-end had holes?*
>
> *Have you figured out a way to mitigate that risk at Acme corp? Our machine-learning based cipher enriches your firewall protection by 62% protecting against similar breaches: worth exploring?"*

And now here's the template you can use:

> Did you notice/know/have you heard of <NEWS> about <LOSS/PAIN> because <WHAT AVATAR IS NOT DOING>?

Have you figured/What are you doing to avoid <LOSS> at <COMPANY NAME>?

Our solution does X to achieve <DESIRED OUTCOME>

Worth exploring?

While it may seem vague, this template has teeth because it's a fear/pain emotional resonance heuristic. The cybersecurity company mentioned above leveraged a clear fear for their target audience: the fear of getting their servers breached by ever-sophisticated hackers using AI.

TROUBLESHOOTING

I've spent countless dollars and staff-hours A/B testing over 5 million emails for 100 concurrent clients. Through this work, I've recognized some of the biggest issues people have with sending cold emails.

In the same vein, I encourage you to A/B test the concepts in this book. And when you're done, A/B test some more. If you find your strategy still isn't working, contact me and I'll see if I can help you refine it.

Often, when clients do come to me, suggesting the JMM strategies don't work for their vertical, all they've needed to do is make a couple of basic tweaks. Hence why it has legitimately driven billions in qualified pipeline for tens of thousands of sellers everywhere.

Most of the time, "brevity" fixes the majority of messaging issues. Because let's face it, most emails are just too damn long.

I know it's difficult to cut down your messages. As a benchmark: once your marketing team is railing against them, they're actually the right length.

The second biggest issue sellers face, alongside overly-long emails, is nailing the Pain/Fear emotional resonance heuristic. This is the key to triggering both the left and right hemispheres of the brain.

In any comms channel be it voice or digital, prospects buy on emotion and justify their purchases with logic. This means you need to address both areas in rapid succession.

We pique interest with emotion, then help prospects rationalize agreeing to take the meeting with logic, e.g. analyst statistics and ROI proof points. People "love to buy but hate to be sold."

All most salespeople are missing is:

1) telling a story (before/after)
2) dialing up pain-fear emotional resonance with emotional phrases like: • challenged by • struggling with • stressed out about • losing sleep over • overwhelmed • irritated by • frustrated with • couldn't figure out how to • tearing their hair out • hemorrhaging money

A note on reply management:

1) ALL REPLIES are positive
NEGATIVE responses are a sign of interest too

2) Handling replies with psychology tactics can create a boomerang effect where you can still get a meeting 3-5 days later or next quarter.

If a prospect replies: "This isn't relevant to me." I'd reply, "What would make this relevant?" If they say, "We're not in the market right now." Reply with, "Just curious, when will you be in the market?" Use softeners that are empathetic and conciliatory like, "I totally understand" or "That's fine," even "Makes sense," in reply.

One of the best terms you can use in sales is: "Just curious."

Sometimes I say this 25X on a call. Who doesn't like a curious person?

Here's one leveraging the Opinion Heuristic: "Can you please coach me on how I could have made this more relevant to you?" It's a similar move to admitting you're falling on your sword.

After sending 5 million emails, the theory is, if they respond at all, you're already opening a dialogue. Find a way to get more info.

Remember, rejection emails are an excellent opportunity to ask for a referral too.

Ask who your prospect knows who could benefit from your solution, or who else you might be able to contact in their organization. "Can you please have the courtesy to point me in the right direction to whoever handles this?"

The psychology here is not to outsmart them but dig to the real objection. Take the response: "Let's talk in 6 months." The bold rep challenges this, "What's going to change in 6 months?" "We don't have the budget now." "No worries, when will you have the budget?" Fortune favors the bold and you can boomerang nearly any written rejection if you're inventive enough.

If open rates remain under 20%, you probably have a RevOps issue with your security protocols: DKIM, DMARC, SPF, or DNS record. You may have blown your deliverability, sender score, domain health or be on some kind of blacklist. You might be sending on the root domain vs. a subdomain. Possibly even into a honeypot, a fake e-mail address to trap spammers.

SDRs who came before may have sent 300 emails per day when the new Gmail caps are 50 per day. There are lists of 400 spam words. There are people that swear by personalizing every last message or using Spintax to throw off the syntax of emails (so they appear slightly different every time to the spam filters).

I've visited with the majority of the world's leading experts on this subject and the consensus is clear:

Stick to the basics to maintain your authority.

Your email signatures should never include spammy links, even a picture link to your next conference – please, no links of any kind. Also never introduce yourself with a sales title: Account Executive, Sales Development, VP, Sales. Here's an example of my signature that spam arrays like / let through:

Justin Michael
Strategic Accounts
Acme
+1 917.232.2164

That's it!

Write high-quality emails relevant to your audience. Provide them with valuable, engaging content that they actually want to read. It solves all the other problems if your domain is clean and slowly warmed up.

(Google: The Definitive Checklist for Sending Cold Emails by Raj Nadar)

In closing, re-sequence your prospect every 3 to 6 months depending on how assertive you'd like to be or how conservative your industry is.

GPT Lab: Subject line writing

Practicing writing subject lines for emails is a powerful skill.

Here are a few prompts to help you practice writing subject lines:

1. "You are a world-class communicator who writes award-winning emails. What catchy and attention-grabbing subject line ideas will encourage B2B buyers to open my email and explore my offering?"
2. "How can I create personalized and engaging subject lines that resonate with B2B buyers and demonstrate an understanding of their needs?"
3. "What are some proven strategies for writing subject lines that spark curiosity and showcase the unique value proposition of my solution to B2B buyers?"

Social Selling via Chat (4th Frame)

The 4th Frame will revolutionize B2B outbound over the next decade especially as ChatGPT is programmed to do it. The scary piece of GPT is when you program it for empathy + casual content. It really sounds human to me.

> *"You can make more friends in two months by becoming interested in other people than you can in two years by trying to get other people interested in you."*
>
> *– Dale Carnegie*

Chat and grow rich.

Said no one, ever. But it's possible with the JMM. Oh really, how?

No matter what anyone promises you, none of these motions predictably drive high quality clients with a short sales cycle:

1. Marketing
2. Advertising
3. Social posts
4. Branding
5. Niching

What does? Real-time (RT) conversations. You can build an empire by slowing down and just having high quality chat conversations all day. I've done it!

As a CEO (of your own territory) or Founder, traditional prospecting methods often lower your power/status frame and come off as needy, then inadvertently repel prospects.

First remember this: the green dot means they're online.

Second, you must realize that Linkedin is not an email platform, it's about interactive chat flows. I used to believe you could manually sequence it, but then at 52K followers and 30K direct connections, a major lightbulb went off. "If I'm directly connected to thousands of ideal buyers, why can't I unlock immediate business opportunities?"

Just like emails need to look like text messages, LinkedIn messaging needs to be approached as chat. Think micro-messages like dance steps back and forth in threads - not long emails; not dropping calendly links.

Imagine you are at a TEDx conference, Davos or Salesforce World Tour and you bump into someone you vaguely know on LinkedIn. Would you push your business card? Would you talk formally or in bullet points? Never!

You might say, "Hey, what did you think of that Tony Robbins talk?" You'd be human, curious, and interested...

Bump into people in your feed now (just like in real life at the grocery store), strike up conversations, focus on them, be human and curious. That's the bedrock mindset of 'the 4th frame.'

LinkedIn is the most underutilized asset because everyone to this day just "pitch slaps." Connect, pitch. There's no seduction - no rapport anymore.

We assume just because we have a first-degree contact on our list, we don't have to connect on a deeper level. However, fail to connect with your prospect as a human being, and you could be missing out on amazing opportunities.

Conversations in "DMs" should feel just like discussions in real life. They should consist of a number of intricate dance steps, chosen to align you with your conversational partner.

Rather than obsessing over how you can personalize every message as much as possible, focus on actually having a real, authentic conversation.

In today's world, human-style conversational communication can be synthesized by GPT tools. But the heart behind the conversation is missing. ChatGPT can't deliver humor, wit, sarcasm, and empathy like humans can - at least not for now.

The "Fourth Frame" for sales is nestled within the evolving social selling landscape. It's essentially the process you use to pull more value from LinkedIn and Sales Navigator - but it will work on any DM platform, from WhatsApp, to SMS and Instagram.

For years, sellers have been searching for a "magic bullet" template guaranteed to drive replies on social media. What I've done is A/B test an elaborate series of real-time chat interaction frameworks step by step to unlock your chat flows once and for all.

Plenty of magic can happen within your DMs, but 999 out of 1,000 sellers damage their relationships with first-degree connections with an immediate pitch. Pitch slapping is expected; even if you wait to do it, the prospect still sees right through your thinly veiled attempts at rapport building and suddenly/permanently goes dark.

So, how do we flip the script?

First, a history lesson: Since Alexander Graham Bell invented the phone in 1876, salespeople have been learning how to use communication tools to solicit with them. Heck, consumers still get those pesky sales calls at dinnertime to this day, whether it's legal or not.

Then email came along in the '90s and it was soon abused with the advent of spam cannons. The government regulated both calls and emails with the Do Not Call (DNC) list and the CAN-SPAM act. And now we have GDPR hysteria too.

Folks like Brian Tracy got slick in the '90s and figured out it would be a cute parlor trick if you just "closed them on time" vs. selling a product. Meaning - your first "close" is getting them to agree to give their time. But prospects have cottoned on. They're wise to the old sales games, and they no longer work.

Hence the ubiquity of the phrase, *"Can I get 15/30 minutes of your time Tuesday or Thursday?"* This should be banned from prospecting. When you're asking for anything from a prospect, even time, you need to show them what's in it for them. In other words, you need to deliver value first.

In 2007, I invented Route-Ruin-Multiply (RRM) as a call opening framework. It worked because 30% of the time, your data is bad due to job changes and layoffs. You could get instant internal referrals vs. the usual "not interested, send info" response and endless gatekeeping.

Side note: "Send info," is the kiss of death, and usually it's untrue. "Buyers are liars" so this is really a brush off into the circular file.

Never settle for this answer, just become better at prospecting so you don't hear it. If you do get it, say:

"Every time I've sent info, that prospect has left me for dead. Are you really telling me you're never going to speak to me again?" Then laugh.

(See Objection Handling section)

History of outbound:

1. First Era - sell product
2. Second Era - sell time
3. Third Era - sell ROUTE (matrixed) – the JMM 2007
4. Fourth Era - converse – the JMM 2022

The 4th Frame technique expands on the real-time 1st and 2nd-degree messaging capabilities on channels like LinkedIn. The big challenge is getting enough dry powder to start threads. At the time of this writing, there's a loophole in Sales Navigator I reverse-engineered from LI-automation platforms like Skylead.io.

600 million messages later and Mailshake confirms, "LinkedIn messages are less flooded than email inboxes, which results in an impressive reply rate of 5-20%." LinkedIn always stated InMail was 3X more effective than email but if you only send 50 messages per month, you'll never see the results yourself.

You can immediately get *800 InMails* by right clicking and checking for the green badge 'open profiles.' (At this writing, they may have removed the green badge but if you hit message, you can still see "open profile" inside the message pane.) Set the advanced 'lead filters' search settings in Sales Nav under 'spotlights' to 'changed jobs in the last 90 days' or 'posted in the last 30 days'. If they accept any InMail, you can ping them multiple times or "bump" responders which allows you to perfect your follow-ups. Create a Lead Filters search.

Catch 2nd degree, function, seniority, spotlights - posted on LinkedIn and make sure to exclude "people you've interacted with or messaged" under the 'workflow' section. This ensures when you save that list, every time you reload it daily, there are fresh contacts to reach.

Again, freshness and recency generates the conditions for a much higher likelihood of response. If a zombie profile prospect never logs in or posts, your chances of starting a good conversation are practically non-existent.

You need to find these high-intent targets one at a time, unless you use automation like Skylead.io or SelfDisrupt to do this, but the daily cap can be lower (~40). The flaw in LinkedIn automation is if you send messages too fast, your profile gets shut off, aka the dreaded "LinkedIn Jail."

Additionally, LinkedIn targeting is generally spotty, so don't rely on it completely.

Bring your own brain into the process. It's a supercomputer all on its own, with a unique ability to pattern match and make judgments based on past experience. This means your brain is more powerful than all the supercomputers in the world strung together - at least for now. Google's new quantum computer at the time of this writing may have just jumped the shark.

Slow down and be the snail; target people one by one. Never waste an invite or InMail again. Then if anyone responds, it's a dream prospect. Use a spear gun for targeting, not a lobster net.

So, what should you put in an InMail?

Follow the copywriting heuristics throughout this book and use a tight SPEAR (reach out for *Codex 9-11*):

Subject line: Growth (1-3 words, action word, Picasso angular)
Subject line 2: Name + fraud analytics
Body: Hey Name, Based on how we successfully helped Acme, Beta & Zeta reduce fraud by 36% w/ our proprietary algorithm and 16 data scientists on staff, we could be doing a lot with Your Co. worth exploring?

Leverage reciprocity by attaching a "high value/utility" PDF to your message. Give to get. Do you have a cheat sheet or guide that's immediately useful to solve a problem or help a prospect achieve their goals?

One word of caution: do not exceed more than 75 messages outbound per day combined from both standard LI and Sales Navigator. If you do, you risk your profile getting shut off or sent to LI jail. And don't forget to bump those 75. When you bump them, give away a guide, a PDF, a cheat sheet, or a checklist to trigger reciprocity. Nobody is following up effectively on LinkedIn; the vast majority send just one touch and then "check out."

Outside of that, always consider your circle of 'first connections' as it frequently reveals itself to be a goldmine. Ask yourself these two questions:

1. "How many 1st degree connections do I have?"
2. "Of those, how many do I think could be customers?"

Usually, there are thousands of connections you can leverage, and hundreds of potential customers waiting in the wings.

So, why waste your time seeking out perfect strangers who might just happen to be the perfect fit for your business?

Start with your first-degree inner circle; radiate out from there.

Mine your first circle of friends and past colleagues that know, like and trust you on LinkedIn *first* using the 4th frame to build an immediate client base. Mine your cell phone for relevant people you can directly message, too.

I think one of the reasons people are afraid to mine the first degree, is they fear "rejection" from people they actually know more than from people they don't. They have an irrational fear they'll be ridiculed by their peers, former colleagues, friends or family. So ask your closest people, "who they know that fits the profile" of your dream client. Then they can self-select if they themselves have the problem. You're in the wrong profession if you don't want to be bold and ruffle some feathers.

Now, let's dive straight into it.

THE FOURTH FRAME

"Before the mastermind even started, JM shared the magic of the 'fourth frame.' In 20 minutes I learned more about sales psychology and LinkedIn prospecting than I had in the last 3 years.

2 hours later, I booked a disco call using his methods. Within 3 days I drove 80K in pipeline just chatting... That says it all really.

He's a Jedi. And a lovely, caring dude who cares deeply about serving others." – Luke Shalom, Founder, Grow Solo Media

It's all going down in the DMs.

Mastering your DMs is like learning a series of simple tango steps you can use whenever you have a real-time interaction on LinkedIn, Instagram, Twitter, WhatsApp, or even in person.

You stay:

1. Focused on their problem/opportunity
2. Curious about their world / their profile
3. Ready to become a part of their future (inject your solution)

Just fixate on 1 and 2 back to back until they crack, and polarity shifts. There's no rocket science here. Embrace detective, doctor, and therapist archetypes (hat tip Jeff Thull). Resist your impulse to impress or show off.

Follow these exact steps to unlock the polarity shift in your direct messages (DMs). If you do it right, they'll take an immediate call or you can drop your calendly. Safe crack.

The risk is to be so personalized and "chatty" that you get "friend zoned." You must make sure to hit #3 and "insert your solution." The risk of quick rapport building is you have a great DM chat but it never materializes into a Zoom call or real business.

Before I dive in explaining why this model works, here's the overall structure below.

1. Connect/InMail
2. Starter Thread
3. Lateral Ask
4. Challenges + thread sparker
   a. Yes -> 'relate' + peel onion layer
   b. No -> Move to step 5
5. Goals + thread sparker

      a. Yes -> 'relate' + peel onion layer
6. Give
      a. Share insight, content, testimonial
7. Past solutions + thread sparker
      a. "What have you tried before?"
8. Personal story, lightbulb moment, your solution
9. Light ask
      a. "Wanna see if we can help you with that?"

Addressing a challenge is essential to a valuable sales conversation.

If you can't find a challenge or goal, relate with vulnerability or empathy. Remember Jill Konrath's Paradox, "To be consultative, be assumptive." You're better off assuming and getting it wrong, and graciously letting prospects correct you, than to go in blank like, "What's keeping you up at night?"

1:1 chat flows are intimate, so the same mechanics do not govern them as 1:many, a cold call (stranger intruding), or a cold email. You need to remain highly humble and generous. Remember to use emojis to soften and impact the implied tonality of a chat, especially if delivering something that may be misconstrued as hard feedback or negative.

If you focus on their problem (give) and are genuinely curious (love = give), you'll end up with a customer.

At the very least, you'll have someone willing to communicate with you further. Then you can pull your prospect right out of the chat flow into a live Zoom call. It's wildly efficient. Go chat with a prospect right now in your feed, and hop on a call immediately. Why wait? Why sequence for 6 weeks? Generate business now: in quality conversations.

Strong salespeople are overtrained on steps #1 and #3 above and forget to build rapport throughout the interaction. Without true human connection, strong sellers seem too slick and glib on DMs.

Then there's the "personalization" crowd who love to talk about sports and triathlons all day. That puts them in the friend zone penalty box and they can never really transition to closing the deal. Many have embraced the dangerous "personalization at scale philosophy" and come off creepy or cheesy. "You love hiking? So do I, wow! Let's hike right up the revenue mountain to the peak of forecasting excellence." Delete.

Executives don't want to have a steak dinner with their vendor. They want you to improve their earnings and results so they can spend more time with the people they love, doing those hobbies you're so keen to talk about.

"Money follows value so add value first." – Brian Ellwood

Putting it in another way:

1. Provoke, *then* listen
2. Provoke, *then* listen (yes, it repeats)

The more you listen, the more they'll feel heard. The act of giving creates a polarity shift.

Now they're interested in you — from that new openness of intent, the sale opportunities spring eternal.

Deep curiosity and deep listening generates intrigue.

Keeping the conversation flowing starts with asking powerful, open-ended questions. But which ones?

Be even more curious and those questions will flow naturally from you.

You don't have to master SPIN. Be a true detective. Be fascinated. Make them the most interesting person who ever lived on this Earth. Find out everything you can possibly know about them.

Slow. Way. Down. Remember, you're now forever a happy little garden snail. The more time you invest up front in building the relationship, the bigger the deal and higher likelihood of close. One-call close? Radically, take 3-6 - if it's your dream client, that's nothing!

And by provoke I mean "produce interest." If they don't respond to a single lower case phrase or sentence, you're not provocative enough yet. If you send a quick ping – no pleasantries – in a DM and get nothing back, should you give up? No! Keep A/B testing. Your messages might lack an answer to that all-important question:

"What's in it for me?"

Focus on their world: their pains, problems, challenges, goals, dreams, opportunities, secret fears, and irritations. Walk a mile in their shoes. Provoke. What's more powerful in this world than the force of fear or love? Curiosity.

When it's real and you give all your focus in the now to just one soul. That tractor beam, that Bat Signal, that Care Bear Stare heartlight, changes everything in prospecting - it's unstoppable; limitless.

You'll become a limitless lead magnet converting every conversation into something worthwhile - a relationship is built, then a referral, then a reciprocal flywheel of caring and serving one another. It's why all modern selling is broken and backwards, it's medieval. It's all about *taking*. It MUST become about *giving* for you. Read *Go-Giver*, pay it forward and serve.

Even if you lose the sale, you gain relationships, expand your network, and open up new opportunities. People just discard each other now, a disqualified lead in some plastic 'transactional' funnel. It's almost barbaric.

1,000 years ago, you were the town blacksmith so you made swords, and if you did a good job, knights came from miles around to buy them from you. Maybe you made a few marauders extra sharp, light ones, the word got out, and then your dance card was full. The metaphor is obvious:

The best way to build up a business isn't marketing, advertising, social media and endless "look at me" needy/creepy behavior. It's to show up at someone's front door, start painting their house (even for free) in an excellent fashion. Then, the neighbor sees it and asks, "Who painted this?" and hires you. Then you have a client. Major hat tip to John Patrick (JP) Morgan Jr. on this analogy. We gain clients faster by freely delivering excellence. Let them experience the value of being your customer from the first interaction. Act as if they already are.

"And at what point does being a detective become creepy?" - you might ask.

It's the platinum rule, "do unto others as you believe THEY'd like to be treated." Not *you*. That's where the golden rule falls down and why so many people repel their prospects. It's so easy to focus on yourself with phrases like:

- I advise Elon Musk
- I make 2MM bucks
- We're top right on the Gartner grid

All that doesn't work for [thing you do] because prospects don't want to be another notch on your bedpost. Hence that's why intimacy is a key component of The 4th Frame.

In fact, DMs are an often abused, private thing so the trust levels need to be crazy high. What you'll find with these senior people is nobody has listened to them or tried to help them (genuinely, without ulterior motives) for 20 years.

They've come up as alpha dogs out there, like a lone wolf at the top of the heap in the cold and rain. Their spouses don't listen to them, nor do their bosses. They report exhaustively to a faceless board and shareholders. What's the one locus of control they do have? Their P&L.

You should always focus on two key factors:

- Focus on their problem (give)
- Be genuinely curious = love (give)

If you keep on that long enough and then slip into that stream, you've got yourself a client.

A big mistake I see sellers make is trying to jump right into fixing the problem. Or, immediately challenging for "Challenger" sake. Even jumping right into SPINning it and peeling the onion.

Instead, show empathy and relate to them with your own story. My protegé Luke Shalom is a wizard at creating empathy and has iterated endlessly on the core 4th frame chat flow technique. When we run the fourth frame, we share our struggle. Something to the effect of:

"Hey I get it, I was struggling building my brand (tell your personal, vulnerable story), and then I created this method and turned it around."

In this book, I'm constantly sharing my own stories, covering failures and successes, to help you relate to me. The same concept applies to first calls, discovery and in advanced chat flow interactions. Empathy is a superpower. But it requires vulnerability and that takes courage.

Say a prospect confides in a DM, "I'm struggling with X or Y," and you respond with high EQ, "I totally relate, I used to struggle with that too... Example."

In the words of star protegé Luke Shalom:

> "I have booked $80k of pipeline in three days just by relating to their pain points."

And, if you don't know where to start, here's a huge step-by-step hack for you to turn 'em all into sales conversations:

1. Monitor who likes your posts
2. Scan for your ICP (executives)
3. Connect and open the conversation with an open question: "thanks for liking my post, how's work?" An appreciation heuristic will work till the year 3,000.
4. Ask open ended questions related to:
   a. Their problem / their solution
   b. Personal facts on their profile
5. Alternate between the two until prospect polarity shifts (cold to hot).
6. You will know you have them interested when they ask "how" do you get a certain result or "how much?" an early buying signal
7. Position yourself as the viable solution.

Result: unlimited sales conversations with people who already *trust* you.

Consultants 4th Frame (alternate):

1) Identify a problem
2) Peel it to the root
3) Start advising in the thread
4) Pull them to a "brainstorm" call

The theory is if they're getting real value and you decrease time to value - TTV - from the first interaction, they'll pay for more. Make sure you help and advise from go. This leaves your prospect thinking, "Wow, this Justin guy is already helping me, he's going to be even more valuable as a coach."

"But I can't get people to chat with me, JM? What should I write first?" The key is to use a lower case single sentence as an opener, and get creative in making an indirect ask to kick off threads:

1. how are things over at Acme?
2. are you seeing headwinds in the recession? (lateral macro trend ask)
3. what impact do you think ChatGPT will have on SEO? (lateral micro trend)

Another fantastic indirect question sounds like this, "Hey Name, I can see you're pretty connected; who do you know who is struggling with marketing automation challenges right now?" The beauty of this one is they can self-select, "Oh, actually that sounds like me." Or, make the referral immediately. Normally, you're selling against incumbents anyway.

Warning, you will suddenly be booking three Zoom meetings a day straight out of threads so you need to apply the next advanced level of 4th frame: prequalification to ensure you're not overwhelmed.

Pre-qualify in chats and emails. If you let the chat flow linger, they'll ask the cost and you can broach it with an option of three choices à la Alan Weiss. It's better to determine instantly that your prospect can't afford anything, than to agree to another "free strategy session" Zoom call and come up with zero.

I realize this flies in the face of many coaches that believe in giving an "experience of coaching" with "taster sessions" but I just find too many people will exploit your goodwill not taking chat flows as seriously. So no free consulting!

Remember to be clear about your intentions to create a customer and "ask for the meeting!" Get out of your chat flows into Zoom at the perfect moment. You'll get a feel for this "Goldilocks zone" over time. Strike when the iron is hot. Not too early or late. Use a simple finessed ask, "Perhaps I could help you with that?" or "Should we hop on a quick call to brainstorm this?" Or, if you get resistance, "Isn't it worth at least a quick Zoom chat to see if I can help you with this?"

Luke Shalom has found the 4th frame to be a "meta-framework for persuasion, not simply sales." You can use it for PR – getting booked on podcasts – or as a golden thread in your discovery/ qualification process on the first call itself.

Traditional sales frameworks all look alike:

1. Probe (find pain)
2. Tailor solution
3. Close

Or still Linear:

1. Rapport build
2. Probe
3. Tailored pitch / product demo
4. Next step

The problem is there is either:

- No real rapport built or
- Rapport building only happens at the front of the sales process

You need to find points of rapport all throughout the first conversation. The classic relationship builder over-indexes on the "personalization" or "rapport building" stuff: "Wasn't that hockey game last night epic?" Prospects feel like, "you must not be too confident in your solution, you just want to be my buddy."

It's YOUR fault they're exploiting your time.

The strong seller is a master at probing, positioning their unique value proposition (UVP) and closing for next steps. But the risk now is that prospects struggle to trust slick sellers.

You must master how to sell without selling. Really think about that phrase and your head might explode, or you just might see that sales are only always created in powerful conversations.

> *"Go deeper than they've ever gone before to find their secret dream." – Rich Litvin*

Pluralism ruins prospecting — "I just need to go get a bunch of clients."

Instead, slow down and focus on the person right in front of you, right now. The person at the top of your social stream (with a problem you can solve). They feel it when you're fully there and present in the conversation, rather than just doing mass target practice.

That's why, when I work with people, it's 100% customized and bespoke. Nothing is a "course" in my world, well not in a traditional sense, even if I package it up that way.

I work with one person at a time like no one else exists. I bring 20+ years of experience to cracking one case. That's why I can charge one of the highest premiums for B2B coaching.

That's why I don't scale. What I tell sellers that aspire to be 7-figure earners, or sellers that are looking to side hustle into coaching, or coaches looking to hit 50K/mos:

> *"Do the unscalable. Slow down to speed up. Get one client, then another. It builds from there."*

I love Jacco Van Der Kooij's concept of even, 'stackable revenue bricks.' Keep your products or services dead simple and go for quality clients over quantity. Remember Pareto in all things: less is more, more with less.

Start now. Here's your new 55 Minute LinkedIn Daily Prospecting Workout:

- 25 invites per day (without a note to create mystery). *You get 100/wk or 400/mo at this writing; used to be way more.*
- If someone accepts; drop a video from the LinkedIn Mobile App (see my Video Prospecting framework)

- 40 InMails per day with your value prop to Open Profile green badges (remember your get 800/mo.)
- Watch carefully who views you, who likes your content Message them any way you can w/ a spear "thanks for liking my carousel, how's life?"
- Spend time liking posts, endorsing skills (pick weird ones they don't expect), interacting with posts meaningfully commenting, and referencing the content - even on Sales Navigator via 2nd degree and on company pages. You'll get noticed and grab more profile views you can mine!

On top of that:

1. A/B test everything: subject lines, first line, CTAs, etc.
2. Interact w/ prospects' posts both 1st and 2nd degree + in their 'recent activity' section - it creates even more views which you can mine.
3. Power move to jumpstart your feed while you ramp: Immediately follow 200 dream prospects (no limit!), curate your feed, and comment. If they view you or comment back, engage.

Because your portfolio of daily, proactive prospecting touches is so crucial, I'll beat the dead horse and hammer home the point.

Said in another way, even more SIMPLY:

1. You consistently add prospects, aka the best ones you can find - 25 per day, Est. time: 15 min
2. You look at who recently added you - you message them all in a single session to try to spark chats - time: 15 min

3. You go to your saved Sales Navigator search and send your "high relevance" template to 40 open profiles who've posted recently or changed jobs - time 25 min

The bedrock of setting up the 4th frame is strategic content creation; optimizing your linkedin profile from a resume to a highly-converting landing page.

Every day, check out everyone that views you and message them either 1st or 2nd degree. That freshness and recency is the strongest buying signal: they took the time to research you back - even if they didn't respond. Act on that signal! (It's so dead obvious but very few people do this.)

Then produce provocative, insight driven - even polarizing, posts in the form of polls, carousels, shared PDFs, and videos that attract your buyers. That will allow you to mine your likes, comments, shares, and profile views as this content generates more interest. See the flywheel?

That's where you need a Jedi like Luke Shalom or Tim Dodd to help you ghostwrite and build out this content for you. Polls are a great way to create polarity around key issues and rapidly get a bunch of votes. You can then mine the specific answer categories as you message poll-takers.

Last hidden trick; if you have no one to talk to, sort the feed by "Recent" and start convos now.

EXAMPLE SIMPLE 4TH FRAME CONVO:

JM: hey marco, how are things over at Acme?

MB: good, thanks – you?

JM: great, what are you focused on in Q2 (or 'this fiscal')?

MB: well, I want to raise our revenue because our SDRs aren't making calls

JM: don't we all, what are your specific challenges?

MB: call reluctance, reps not holding C-Level conversations, lack of organization and acumen, tech stack adoption

JM: I totally get that, been a VP of Sales in companies where they expect a miracle and underfund all the enablement initiatives

JM: ok, what are your goals for the year?

MB: to double the business

JM: ok, what have you tried so far to do it?

MB: we brought in a RevOps consultant and stood up a tech stack but there hasn't been any training

JM: ever work w/ a coach?

MB: no, we can't allocate budget for that

JM: makes sense, but what if it sped you up toward doubling the business? I mean it's a Catch-22, if you invest you could gain

MB: good point, but they even slashed my L&D budgets

JM: what's your goal behind the goal of hitting that milestone?

MB: I want to make the team successful so I can hit my number and get more work-life balance plus travel more

JM: OK, what else have you tried?

MB: I've enrolled everybody in a random course right now, it was cheap but it's just not working

JM: OK, well what would success have looked like?

MB: again, doubling the business

JM: haha

JM: I totally understand what it's like, I had a business churning at 40% and it was only after I built my own methodology that it started turning around

JM: what if there were a way to shortcut your ability to double, based on how I'm helping similar folks accelerate this (happy to share testimonials)

– soft CTA – Do you think I could help you with that? Up to brainstorm on a quick zoom?

TROUBLESHOOTING THE 4TH FRAME:

During your conversation, you're bound to make some promises, and your customers are going to ask you how you're going to deliver those results. Answer that question with a calibration question, "Well, what are you focused on in Q2?"

The other issue I see is people are chatting too long in DMs and the prospect reacts exasperatedly, "Why do you keep asking open questions, what do you *really* want from me?" Make sure to get to Zoom after 2-3 back and forths once polarity flips and they seem interested.

You need to show vulnerability. It's not enough to just get prospects to open up professionally (about challenges) and personally about unique things about their career history. You need to tell the story of how you failed and now leveraged this product, service, or method to succeed so they see themselves in you.

But where can I find prospective customers and clients to run the 4th frame on?

It's staring you right in the face. Just scroll your feed for people you can help now, look for the little green circle they're online, and reach out. Why wait? Create a conversation and a client now. Sure beats doomscrolling.

Once you're done, print out your emails and look for problems you can solve. Rifle through your cell phone contact list and look for people you can reconnect with that you can directly help or are connectors to other customers/clients. Run Sales Nav searches on your own 1st degree and start up threads. (The First Circle)

OPTIMIZING YOUR LINKEDIN PROFILE

Salespeople are often insecure about their ability to write. After all, we're not *all* authors. However, you don't have to be a best-seller to write well. You already have the incredible communication skills a great writer needs. You already communicate powerfully and brilliantly all day: on presentations, demo calls, and discos (discovery calls). Use these skills to enhance your LinkedIn profile, and you'll be more likely to convert the prospects that land on it.

Your headline is your unique value proposition. Instead of 'Account Executive', use this template (h/t Marco Basile):

- *We help [niche] achieve [outcome] within [timeframe] without [pain point/undesirable situation] using [bespoke framework] with [guarantee]*

After that, you can start boosting your profile's potential with the following steps:

1. Share text-based testimonials in your summary
2. Share video testimonials in your 'featured' section
3. Rewrite your work history from the viewpoint of the buyer

Marco Basile, an expert in closing tactics and a framework editor for this book, has been kind enough to share two templates that you can immediately use to make your LinkedIn summary shine. Here they are below:

Headline:

{{UVP}}

Summary:

As the {{role}} at {{company}}, I specialize in {{UVP}}.

Have you found yourself spending most of your time:

- Wrong strategy they put in place #1

- Wrong strategy they put in place #2

- Wrong strategy they put in place #3

As {{avatar persona}}, our {{custom framework}} allows you to:

dream outcome/situation #1

- ✔ dream outcome/situation #2
- ✔ dream outcome/situation #3
- ✔ dream outcome/situation #4

I'd like to show you how we do this and how you can leverage our {{custom framework}} to {{achieve outcome}}.

>>> Let's book a call and let me walk you through our processes and show you how you can execute the {{custom framework name}}.

→ \<LINK TO CASE STUDIES>

Keyword #1 | Keyword #2 | Keyword #3

Headline:

{{UVP}}

Summary:

{{UVP}}

- Company name #1, achievements
- Company name #2, achievements
- Company name #3, achievements

On top of sheer results, we provide you with X guarantee.

This is NOT for everyone though.

Here are our conditions:

- Qualifier #1
- Qualifier #2
- Qualifier #3

If this sounds like you, then you and I need to talk.

Send me a DM here.

If you cannot wait, book a time with me here for a discovery call:

\<YOUR LINK>

When I work with sales executives around the world, they wonder why their LinkedIn invite acceptance rate is low. The reason is often simple: when people view their profile, they see no value save for a "sales professional seeking to get hired." So, they bounce. Here's what you can do to change that:

1. Optimize your profile according to your value prop and target audience
2. Publish posts once/day, including polls
3. Mine posts likes and comments
4. Strike up conversations with people that follow you and view you
5. Interact with your prospects via 2nd degree in Sales Navigator by commenting on their posts, and leveraging their posts in personalization
6. Leverage the 4th frame to weaponize your content once you make posts

Want more traffic on Twitter (X) too? Here are some hacks to help with that

1. Change your website URL on Twitter to point to your LinkedIn page
2. Match up the hashtags there — every time you push a LinkedIn post to Twitter, you'll drive even more followers back to LinkedIn.
3. Change your LI connection button from 'connect' to 'follow'
4. Use hashtags to leverage the major content streams that your target audience is consuming to amplify. Get a list of the top hashtags on LinkedIn and Twitter. E.g. #Entrepreneurship and #Innovation have 10s of millions of followers

And don't forget to scan your feed to look for problems and ice-breaker opportunities you can drop into chat threads:

- "Hey, just saw your post, I'm a fan of that Unicorn book too."
- "Hey, noticed you're hiring and just saw your post."
- "Hey, I know someone looking for that job / who can help you with X problem."

Then make 2-3 micro-bumps if you don't get an immediate response. Remember, one bump should contain a GIVE (like an RFP guide, cheat sheet, or ROI calculator.)

The biggest issue I see in LinkedIn prospecting, is lack of follow-up. A huge number of salespeople connect, pitch, and that's it.

Remember, following up doesn't have to happen only on LinkedIn. In fact, I actually recommend using the phone to connect with prospects as you move down the funnel. Call people to say "thanks for the like." Start a conversation about a post you saw them commenting on:

"Hey, I just caught your response on Justin Welsh's post about solopreneurship and thought this would be relevant." This can get amusing. "Calling you up because you viewed my email 27 times." An IT client of mine used this line, got a laugh and closed a deal.

We're tying it all together in this chapter.

Salespeople need to become micro-marketers and then leverage DMs to invest time into their leads.

Formula for creating compelling/viral content (IUV):

- Ideation
- Utility
- Vision (Around the curve)

- ◄ Ideation: How do you build a new idea? You mash-up older ones.
- ◄ Utility: What if every time you go on a podcast, release a blog, or write a status update, it's laced with tactics your audience can use today? You become useful. You become irresistible. Necessary. Trusted. Credible. And the cream of your content rises to the top of any newsfeed.
- ◄ Vision is futurism, innovation and seeing ahead of the curve at least 2-5 years. People want to follow the vanguard - the cutting edge voices in the market.

Blend these 3 ideas in every last piece of communication you put out to the public and you can't lose. You'll be ranked on top influencer lists within a quarter.

Here's a quick tip for commenting on LinkedIn: Provoke. Ask. Provoke. Ask. Empathize. Ask. Be willing to deep comment and string together a few comments to go long form.

Polarize by sharing your real, genuine opinion - provided that it helps people. If you disagree with the masses, be respectful, but confident. Back up what you say with research, and you'll keep the conversation going.

GPT Lab: Create a great Linkedin tagline or summary

GPT has read a lot more Linkedin profiles than you.

It can help you turn your Linkedin profile into a targeted landing page. Here are a few prompts to help you do that:

1. "You are a potential hiring manager. As an accomplished professional, what are the key experiences, skills, and achievements I should highlight in my LinkedIn summary to showcase my unique value and expertise?"
2. "What are some engaging storytelling techniques I can use to make my LinkedIn summary stand out from the crowd and connect with my target audience?"
3. "How can I incorporate specific keywords and phrases in my LinkedIn summary that will optimize my profile for search visibility and attract the right connections and opportunities?"

Video Prospecting (Golden Globes)

"We have worked with Justin for several months to improve our prospecting and sales process. Justin has worked directly with our executive team and Business Development Managers to understand what needs improvement. Justin has improved our process tremendously and increased our prospecting results. I appreciate the hands-on coaching and dedication to getting it right. With his help, we finally have a recipe that we can leverage for repeatable and predictable results. I highly recommend working with Justin to improve your sales process and team's results."

– Benjamin Hicok, COO at Complete Network

I have a breakthrough idea for you via a rep in England. It's subtle, but taken on faith and applied literally it *will* work.

You make a short, raw video on your cell phone. Just record yourself talking to the camera clarifying your business model. Discuss the challenges you solve and how you drive value to customers. Then send that message tailored to each new 1st degree connection you feel is a valid lead.

If "opening is the new closing" per Iannarino, then "a 1st degree connect is the new opening."

Most enterprise leaders and hot startups won't even bother connecting with you on social unless they think you're valuable already. So shake things up a bit.

Sending a video, even a simple one, in that first contact is disruptive. It requires humility, authenticity, and sincerity - and those things drive results. A human face talking to a camera truthfully about the problems they solve will earn you way more meetings than just sending the same old text.

You can build on this strategy too - generating even more value.

Ask yourself: What are the top 1-3 challenges you think you can solve for each customer based on their persona, profile, or background? Put those things into your video, and make it personal.

I've watched an Enterprise rep do this at scale on every new accepted invite and land *unlimited* meetings. There's a nuance here: consistency.

We've all seen sellers experiment with ideas like this sporadically. But how many do it with every single opportunity, using a deliberate formula. Pretty revolutionary right?

Here's a 'Video on Connect' script you can steal:

"Excuse the unorthodox approach:

I'm currently working with major companies X, Y, Z. (Social proof - mention a competitor)

We help companies like [Your Co.] with these three Challenges (use pain-fear heuristics)

1. Challenged by the lack of...

2. Stressed out about problems with...

3. Fed up with...

Up for an exploratory call? Let me know either way."

Just record from your front-facing camera and upload directly to the LinkedIn Message thread from within the standard LinkedIn Mobile App. When you click on a 1st-degree prospect and then click to message, there is a plus sign *only from the mobile app* that lets you record. Do this 50 - 200 times, and the results will surprise you. I can guarantee it.

I called this method "Golden Globes" because there's a secondary part. If they don't respond, send a second video and tastefully joke, "I guess I'm not going to get a Golden Globe for that one." Tasteful humor is your secret weapon for this methodology.

Now don't get me wrong, I'm still a huge proponent of Vidyard, Loom, and myriad other video creators. I love how you can make your head small, narrating in the bottom left corner and fly through their website, even showing them their own LinkedIn profile and noting interesting elements 'a machine wouldn't find.' I just like to use those tools lower in the funnel, after some initial interaction.

The issue is just like clicking away from an email to a white paper or attachment; clicking away to videos is problematic because prospects have trained themselves never to do it. You never know if clicking a link is safe these days.

The beauty of the above technique is the video is playing 'in line' in their inbox on their mobile device (80% of your outreach is seen there) at one click. This is the same reason I create 3-second GIFs in Zight and Gyazo, so prospects can simply watch wow-factor, demo moments playing directly inside their Outlook or Gmail inbox without needing to click away.

You should be dropping voice notes on connect too and they can echo the above or the standard VM template I've shared aka Lee Bartlett's "The English." E.g. "I have a product that's very relevant to your work; do you mind if I tell you a little bit about it? We've helped Acme, Beta, and Xeta drive a 46% margin increase with AI-enabled logistics compression algorithms. Imagine what we could be doing with your company. worth exploring?"

Here are a few other points to keep in mind when diving into video. I know this landscape can feel like a new world to some sales professionals. I've worked myself with various large teams of SDRs all attempting to perfect video prospecting at the same time. A few things seem to work consistently.

Humor works; tasteful humor. Don't be afraid to let your human side show. I mentioned it above, but it's worth driving home. People want human interactions, and human interactions are built on emotion.

I also recommend leveraging editing software when necessary. You don't need to make your videos look like pro commercials. Basic solutions like iMovie can help you make your content look and feel more interesting.

Most reps that build out videos just shoot themselves talking against a beige wall and think it's personalization because they're reading off elements from the prospect's LinkedIn profile. Going beyond the basics will help you to excel in this area. Let your creativity shine through.

I worked with a chatbot software company and the reps that converted would cut back and forth from a chatbot emulator running on a prospect's site, to multiple views of them talking straight to the camera, even with background music. Editing tools can help you to create this unique visual experience, and tailor it to your brand.

What also works is making the video feel real and raw with the right setting. Record from a gym, a coffee shop, or from your car – not while driving! People rarely resonate with "personalized messages" that seem to be mass produced. Choosing a setting that feels "authentic" sends an important message that you're a real person.

Another tip? Get the structure of your message right.

I'm a big fan of Scott Britton's "bandage wound" technique. You "poke the wound" then bandage it with your proposed solution. This works very well in e-commerce and any business prospect that has a website experience you can mystery shop.

You can literally record a video of broken elements on their site and use it as irrefutable proof of why they need to talk to you and make the change. I used this technique in mobile marketing where I'd send screenshots of negative reviews on the app store and tie it to ways our mobile marketing platform could improve workflows and app mechanics. QED is Latin for "thus it is demonstrated."

I'm working with a very gifted enterprise outbound rep who is able to build a 99 page, ROI-focused business case breaking down a cash flow analysis. He thrives in the video landscape by sending a fly-through of this custom report with key highlights circled in red and his face is in the corner narrating it.

He makes assumptions in advance about what CFOs genuinely want to hear about, and then dives in with the visuals. As I've always said, to be compelling, walk a mile in your customer's shoes. Imagine living a day in their life. If you were literally living their life, what would compel you to respond? What would you want to see in a video?

GPT Lab: Create a 30 second script

If you're feeling shy, GPT can help you create a script to engage.

Here's a prompt to try:

"We are being introduced for the first time. Can you ask me a few questions and then provide me with a captivating 30-second introduction script that highlights my key strengths, experiences, and areas of expertise, while also engaging the listener and leaving a lasting impression?"

Visual Prospecting (Venns)

Ignore neuroscience in B2B at your own peril.

Our brains are incredible things. They have the power to take words and transform them into evocative, unforgettable images. As a sales professional, you have the opportunity to be a true neuroscience artist.

Learn how the nuances of the brain work, and you can use your words, your actions, and your strategies to paint a picture that earns your prospect's attention, their trust, and eventually, their investment.

However, you don't have to rely exclusively on your mastery of language.

Today's sales professionals have endless tools at their disposal for this artistic endeavor. You can use videos and visuals in your emails to bring context to conversations, and ignite the synapses of your target audience.

Your knowledge of each prospect you contact, and the solutions or services you offer can help you craft narratives that magically transport the people you contact into new environments and scenarios. The visuals you include alongside these narratives infuse them with additional context, and impact.

You even have the power to manipulate the Limbic system - the emotion center of the brain. Learn how to recognize your customer's emotions, show empathy, and engage through active listening, and you'll discover you can tame, calm, and reassure even the most aggressive prospect.

Appealing to the human mind, and understanding the functioning of the brain, is part of what makes the JMM method so unique.

The brain is essentially a Holodeck and visual processor, constantly responding to different types of stimuli. You may have heard of Oren Klaff's description of the "Croc Brain," an ancient part of the Limbic system.

Essentially, the "crocodile brain" is the most primitive aspect of cognition, and one of the earliest examples of human consciousness to develop. It's the tool that filters the stimuli we encounter every day into categories for "safe" and "dangerous".

The "Croc brain" functions as the triage center of the human mind, deciding what's important for us to pay attention to, and what's "safe" to dismiss. These ancient parts of the brain are still active in our prospects today.

To massage the mind of the modern consumer, we need to learn how all of the components of the brain work together to influence how we act and behave.

The concept of "right brain" and "left brain" people has long-since been debunked. The key to success isn't trying to dance between two different hemispheres controlling emotion, creativity, and logic in different quantities, but learning exactly which regions of the brain control crucial outcomes.

Is taking a psychological, neuroscience-driven approach to sales manipulative? You tell me. I see it as a way of learning how to communicate with your prospects on a distinctly human level. After all, we're all just brains attached to nerves, bones, and muscles on a basic level.

So, how does visual prospecting allow you to connect with the brains of your prospects on a more effective level?

Simple.

If email is really just written symbols translated into imagery in the visual cortex, the big issue with most emails is they're just too bland.

Chunks of text might be informative, but they're not particularly engaging. They don't awaken other synapses in our brains with shapes and color. As salespeople we need to intentionally trigger other parts of the Limbic brain.

Once we've engaged the Limbic system, the Prefrontal cortex then jumps into action, regulating thoughts, actions, and emotions. We can guide this regulatory process with stories, social proof, innuendo, and engaging words that ignite various parts of the mind at once.

Failure to fully understand the prospect's brain is one of the core reasons why cold calling and cold emailing have been fundamentally broken since these mediums began.

Here's how to fix it:

1. Alter your cold calling approach:

Cold calls risk fight or flight (Limbic). Finesse is necessary for calming the triggered Limbic brain. Reduce the sense of danger by creating trust and rapport. Use active listening, empower your prospects to speak, and validate their concerns.

= ROUTE

Simplified: When cold calling intrusions trigger fear - calm down prospects with open questions, empathy, and a transfer of power. Ensure their voice is heard.

2. Avoid boring emails:

Emails are far too rational (stay in the Prefrontal Cortex) and lack visuals (actual) or emotive written narratives. They need to be engineered to go deeper to the older brain. Use diagrams (talk to Product Marketing or make your own) to spark the emotions in the Limbic (amygdala) through storytelling and then calm it down / rationalize via empathy, insight, and quantified value (social proof) to tamp that emotion down.

Simplified: In writing, make someone emotional (unconsciously), then help them to regulate and manage those emotions.

JMM's Visual Thesis: Everything in prospecting is visual, not words. It's all about understanding and leveraging the natural way the prospect's "old" and "new" brain work together.

Let's take this concept into the world of venn diagrams.

Building Venn Diagrams doesn't take a design degree. The simpler, the better; even if you sketch it out on a coffee shop napkin. They also don't have to be perfect. Some of the first diagrams I ever sent to prospects were met with responses like:

"Hey JM, do you realize your diagram is wrong?" That feedback isn't a negative thing.

Remember we are trying to provoke a response. Interactivity is currency. All responses are positive.

The brain processes images at 60,000 times the speed of text. It's true: a picture is worth (at least) a thousand words. The brain also retains visual information for longer, giving you more opportunities to be memorable.

Adding Venn diagrams to your emails and messages can be valuable - when done correctly. It's one of the best ways to engage more of your customer's brain with your conversation. Nest a Venn on the 2nd or 3rd touch, and make sure it's under 1MB to get through the spam filters.

The first Venn I ever sent helped me to set a meeting with the Chief Digital Officer of McDonald's on the first try. The second caused the VP of Mobile at Home Depot to call the phone number in my email signature and exclaim, "OK, pitch me! Whaddya got?"

Image courtesy Travis Pearce

Here's a framework to build fast Venn diagrams:

1. Grab a template for a "3 Circle Venn" from a Google Search - Lucid has good ones.
2. Drop it into a shared Google Slides file as the background.

3. Search for logos in Google image search like: "Acme logo" and under tools pick "transparent" to remove logo backgrounds then just copy/paste.
4. Label 2-3 spheres like Legacy, Point Solution, and Niche to highlight why your product is more robust/expansive or consolidates the other vendors.

A classic Venn makes the case for lowering TCO - total cost of ownership - putting your solution in the middle of the diagram to show it encompasses all the capabilities of the vendors surrounding it. The "one ring to rule them all" consolidation play.

Kyle Rasmussen is an early rockstar of this technique and used to make doodles on napkins and legal pads, or just draw Venns with a BIC pen constantly, sending photos of them to prospects.

This goes to show how simple Venns can be. You don't have to overthink this; the more raw and real, "dust and scratches," the better it converts; just like with unproduced, 'raw' video directly out of the LinkedIn app.

Another really cool Venn variation is putting the customer's logo or even face in the center of a Venn and expressing your solution's relation to their world/ecosystem visually. The way Membrain approached me here to customize my methodology into a CRM is ingenious if you think about it. It's a customer-centric Venn approach - even better!

I've seen advanced applications of Visual Prospecting where personalized images are turned into mini websites in Google and then injected into every email - hat tip to Josh Braun's guide. You could even screenshot visuals from a market research tool like MightySignal to show the monthly active users (MAU) growth counts of apps per account.

This gives the brain access to both engaging visual content, and hard data simultaneously.

I've also seen technical sellers encode emails with Shopify Liquid Syntax. This lets you dynamically change each email automatically per title aimed at, or dynamically change emails by sending code to read the home page of your prospect's site. These applications are very sophisticated.

Your best bet is to think like a Product Marketer does about SEO and SEM. Millions of dollars are already being spent to send visitors to your home page, so take advantage of the assets you already have.

Scour your site and content for pictures that are already converting and put these into your email sequences, LinkedIn messages, and DMs. Make friends with your head of Product Marketing and build a swipe file of the best images.

One of the most advanced techniques is referred to in *Codex 8* as "Flashbang" (hat tip Patrick Joyce, one of my best client testimonials). The idea is to "bump Venns" or in essence, keep bubbling up Venns inside LinkedIn DMs and via email in a flanking motion around the target so the images keep getting forwarded around. This creates enough intrigue and confusion that they take the meeting. "The Art of Confusion" produces responses.

The biggest push back I get on this technique is, "why would I show all my competitors to a prospect?"

Think about it: the minute they decide to seriously evaluate you, they're going straight to Google to find your competitors anyway.

They're then going to interact with these sites, access demos, and research to make sure they get the best deal. By taking the reverse psychology approach above, you simplify your customer's journey, and prime yourself to become the "emotional favorite" as Craig Elias would say. If you trigger an RFP upstream, you can set the requirements.

I sold a mobile push solution once, and our team would show up in Antwerp, Belgium, and on the same day our biggest competitor would be in the lobby with us to take the next meeting.

Anticipate this competitive environment from day one and wire in a Venn Diagram positioning yourself as the leader against the other main logos.

Even if your prospect is already in a sales cycle with a competitor, it pushes them to "reconsider." They'll think: "Wait, I'm seriously considering Beta Corp, maybe we should talk to y'all too? Let's set a meeting."

You are in essence, intercepting 100X the RFPs and existing sales cycle in your segment by displaying deep competitive landscape Venns. That's why it's so important to show logos and not fill your screen with text like "marching ants."

You need to set "traps" and "lock-outs" for competitors you know will be diving into your deal as "column fodder." You need to pre-handle objections if you have an obvious disadvantage or limitation. "Acme was skeptical about upgrading their marketing automation, but then saw HubSpot's ability to do <awesome thing – Josh Braun illumination> so they switched anyway."

Rewire how you look at the "negatives" in your solution compared to the competition. Every potential issue can also be "remarketed" as an advantage. So you're a smaller, bootstrapped company? That just means you can deliver an exclusive, "white glove service".

Maybe you have a specific point solution that doesn't address as many issues as another tool? Well, that just says you're a specialist in your area.

Is your product or service more expensive than whatever your competitor offers? If so, highlight your solution as a premium tool, capable of delivering extra ROI.

Flip every disadvantage into your strength and use every setback as a superpower.

See all selling situations from the viewpoint of advantage.

GPT Lab: Use GPT to create image superpowers

Want to build your own Venn? Use GPT to generate the prompt to use with an image generation tool.

Here's a prompt to try:

"Can you provide a detailed textual description for creating a visually appealing Venn diagram using an image generation tool, with specific instructions on the layout, colors, and labels for each circle, as well as any additional design elements that will enhance the overall presentation?"

You'll need to refine this a bit to include your specific Venn elements, and it will give you an engaging background image.

It's time to take action!

Now that you have read *Justin Michael Method 1.0* and installed your new outbound sales operating system, it's time to take action. Go back over the practical sections in Part IV, and run A/B tests across cold calling, cold emailing, social selling, video and visual prospecting. Go back through the "GPT Lab" sections and test the prompts.

"A/B test everything," as John Barrows loves to say.

Remember that "30 triples per day, keep the performance improvement plan (PIP) away." Your new operating system (OS) is nothing without action, so don't let it be just a bunch of elegant theories that sit on your shelf collecting dust.

Fortune favors the bold.

Hungry for more?

Grab a glass of water, take a moment to adjust, and then come with me on the second half of our journey, in *Justin Michael Method 2.0*.

In the next book, I'll be sharing even more useful insights, such as how to use *The 900 Challenge* to bravely contact 30 new prospects per day, in the next 30 days. We'll cover advanced AI algorithms, negotiation tactics, world class presentations, and even how to maintain your momentum for decades (as I did) in the exhausting world of sales.

Sales is still the greatest profession in the world, and it can be done in a heart-centered way that energizes you and fuels your passion for helping others. The most important thing to remember is that sales is a "sport." It's not a try; it's a *do*.

Stop fearing the "No's" and start actively pursuing them instead. The road to success is paved with more "No's" than you can imagine.

You need to turn up your volume knob for outbound, and crank it to 11, á la "Spinal Tap," until those spiders in the drain rush out. Prospects will no longer be able to hide from you, and you'll be able to give your boss near perfect intel on every account by applying what you learned here in Book 1.

In Book 2, you'll take all the superpowers you've acquired, and enhance them even further. The volume goes from "11" to "infinite." You'll become superhuman.

When I'm coaching reps, the minute they turn up the voicemail knob to 4 or 5 VMs, net new appointments fall like rain. When they finally get organized and are using the Account-Based Sales Development (ABSD) spreadsheet deftly, magic happens. When they're not filling out the "next step" field, they just haven't pressed hard enough with intensity and intention.

The 80/20 rule is constantly working by physics law so ignore it at your peril; you are leaving a wolf at the door. But if you harmonize with account stack ranking and prioritization you'll be working 75% less and 20% of your actions will result in 80% success. Talk about a superpower!

"Be like water making its way through cracks. Do not be assertive, but adjust to the object, and you shall find a way

around or through it. If nothing within you stays rigid, outward things will disclose themselves.

Empty your mind, be formless. Shapeless, like water. If you put water into a cup, it becomes the cup. You put water into a bottle and it becomes the bottle. You put it in a teapot it becomes the teapot. Now, water can flow or it can crash. Be water my friend." – Bruce Lee

Be like the ocean when you prospect. You are the tide and you must keep coming in. *Be relentless.* Eventually, your prospects must react. Don't forget this. If you have 200 key accounts, and you're not setting any meetings, don't just lackadaisically drop in 200 more. Focus harder! Go wider and deeper into that original account base with your relevant sequences, voicemails, and LinkedIn outreach until you get referred or someone says, "No."

For all the hysteria about "personalization at scale," after coaching hundreds of teams, I realized most reps are missing the target because they are far too low on volume. So pick up the damn phone! That's what has made Jeb Blount's *Fanatical Prospecting* such a hit - and why I've recommended it to so many clients. Despite the industry's love affair with sales automation, the weaponization of "spray-and-pray" outbound is failing because we've lost our humanity.

But now it's time to turn the page and go beyond *COMBO Prospecting, Tech-Powered Sales,* and even the *Codices* to *Justin Michael Method 2.0 - The Advanced Operating System.*

We are about to move from the bedrock foundation of the JMM into the most advanced outbound sales prospecting strategies and tactics ever architected and orchestrated. It's time to strap on your jet pack and push the bleeding edge. The next book will tackle advanced GPT prompting and how to scale outbound as an army of one to 2-5X your income and pipeline even faster.

How do you side hustle effectively if you can't possibly hit the income level you seek at your current sales gig? How do you nail every interview, even in the recession? How can you maximize your earning potential and live in prosperity and abundance, staying "in demand" for the rest of your life?

When you make it rain, you become unstoppable and irresistible. Cape is optional. =)

So buckle up, Clark Kent! You're in for a bumpy ride through the Kryptonite asteroid belt of rejection-dense, advanced B2B prospecting now that we've fixed the warp drive and you've mastered the basics of outbound navigation.

The devil's in the details, and the angel's in the marble. So drop everything and get Book 2 now – so you can start carving away, unlocking your inner Michelangelo.

The new you awaits. Your greatest superpower? Belief. I believe in you, so you should, too. As Aaron "AIR" Ross loves to say, "Everyone has a unique genius" when it comes to outbound. And I can attest to this because I've helped thousands become awesome at prospecting.

If you have the will, I can teach you the skill to enter the top 1% of this craft. It's up to you to find it, grab ahold of it, and realize it. Everything you seek is within you. May you never be the same!

I am humbled and grateful for the opportunity to serve you powerfully.

Acknowledgements

THANK YOU:

Julia Nimchinski (GTM Inspiration), Jeremy Jones (Publishing Visionary), Tony J. Hughes (Mentor), Rebekah Carter (Editorial Lead), Nathan Finch (Editor), Greg Meyer (Technical Editor), Marco Basile (Framework Editor), Karan Korpal Sharma (GPT Whisperer), David Youngblood (GPT Whisperer), Soham Sarkar (GPT Whisperer), Scott Martinis (Tech Stack Optimization), Anthony Iannarino, Mike Weinberg, Aaron Ross, Josh Braun, Scott Britton, Max Altschuler, Lars Nilsson, Anders Fredriksson, Steve Richard, Bryan Franklin, Ben Sardella, Marcus Sandberg, Deon Don, Brendan Short, Marcus Cauchi, Jeremey Donovan, Charles Needham, Brian Q. Davis, Moeed Amin, Mark Raffan, Christian Retek, Todd Caponi, Mike Bosworth, David C. Baker, Alan Weiss, Gerry Hill, Jim Holden, Jeff Thull, Mahan Khalsa, Terry Wilson, Josh Braun, Marylou Tyler, Jed Mahrle, Luke Ruffing, Jim Thoeni, Garrett C. MacDonald, Dale Dupree, Stu Heinecke, Jim Mongillo, Colin Sutton, Dennis O'Hagan, Daniel Gray, Steve Chandler, Rich Litvin, Nathan Offner, Barrett Unger, Kellen Casebeer, Bryan Kreuzberger, Ankush Jain, Zach Selch, Victor Antonio, Townsend Wardlaw, Daniel Wax, George Foley, Frank Kohn, Doug McMillen, Nejc Škoberne, Scott Hennessy, Luke Shalom, David Hoffeld, Brian Farrell, Kevin Casey, Randy Stackaruk, Mark Baskin, Gregory Abel, Florian Decludt, Tim Dodd, Marc Periou, Adem Manderovic,

John Smibert, Steven Brady, Dario Junk, Akio Aida, Gunnar Habitz, Benjamin Dennehy, William Wacker, Mike Milewski, Miles Veth, Benjamin Misner, Mike Gallegos, Juan Pablo Garcia, Christopher Rocas, William VanSickle, Michael Koory, Pankaj Sharma, David Catalano, Peter McCammon, Kieran Krohn, Mario Krivokapic, Christian Krause, Darko Davkovski, Eric Steeves, Gavin Tice, Raj Nadar, Aditya Prakash, Joey Gilkey, Cory Bray, Moaaz Nagori

AUTHOR BIO

Justin Michael is a world-record-breaking, outbound sales maven who has arguably built the deepest client acquisition methodology of all time: the Justin Michael Method (JMM). It's driven over 1B in pipeline for 200+ startups he's advised and over 25K reps, 1K of which he's personally coached. Ex Salesforce and LinkedIn, Justin is the global authority on AI-based outbound prospecting alongside legends like Aaron Ross, Josh Braun, and Mark Roberge. His counterintuitive, mobile-responsive, neuroscience-backed visual prospecting methodology made him a million-dollar earner and helped countless startups scale past 10MM ARR. His clients frequently 2-5X their pipeline and income, consistently getting promoted within six months. Justin is the bestselling author of *Tech-Powered Sales*, which proved that over 75% of top funnel can be automated by raising your technology quotient (TQ). He lives in Los Angeles, California, advising top SaaS technology CROs and teams on bleeding-edge revenue models.